The Fight Was Worth It

My Struggles
"The Fight Was Worth It"

By

Keelanashe' T. Armstead

 *The Fight Was Worth It*

This book is printed in the United States of America by Keelanashe' T. Armstead. No material contained in this book may be copied or retrieved in any manner for sale, but may be used in teaching and instruction for the body of Christ.

All Scripture, unless otherwise indicated, is taken from the King James Translation of the Holy Bible.

ISBN- 978-1475018714

Printed in the United States of America

Copyright ©2012 by Keelanashe' T. Armstead

 *The Fight Was Worth It*

Preface

Writing has always been my passion. For me, what I was so passionate about, often told the stories that I was unable to talk about. My purpose for writing this book is to give more of my testimony, and to be a witness to someone that Christ is still performing miracles through His people. He still lives, through us. I hope that something I've written in this book will be an encouragement to you.

Look, no matter what you are going through, no matter what it looks like, no matter what "they say," do not give up. Hold on to God's unchanging hand. I've been there, on the verge of a nervous breakdown and ready to give up. People prayed for me but in the end, I had to pray for myself and it was only Jesus the Christ that brought me through my trials.

However, if you do not have crazy faith, stay in the Word of God. You may not understand what you are reading, but in due season, it will make sense to you. And continue to pray with everything in you. Write down your goals, seek God first for your relationship with Him to grow, and everything else will be added. I want you to know that whatever you endure you are not going through it alone. It may feel like you are all alone but you're not, God's got you, even when it feels like He doesn't. I am also praying for you and love you with the love of Christ.

 *The Fight Was Worth It*

Introduction

Welcome to 'My Struggles' my first book. I am your witty tour guide Keelanashe' '*KeeKee*' Armstead. In this book I will take you on the journey of my life. From time to time you will be greeted with a poem that relates to the story. The poem 'Warning' was written by my nine year old daughter, Kashe'la Armstead. Other times there will be a prayer or Bible text that will follow certain events that happened in my life. I feel as if my Christian life has been like a pregnancy. I dealt with a lot of Braxton contractions. There were times where I thought it would be my season, but God would say not yet. Some days were better than others, but once I started facing various situations I started regretting being a Christian.

My husband would encourage me to keep walking with Christ, because I've come too far to turn around. I noticed that the pain increased the more I walked with Christ. I eventually realized that I needed to be delivered, or I would die with all that rejection towards my Christianity. So, one day as the labor pains intensified, I pushed and pushed, and God allowed me to be delivered of the things that were holding me back from doing God's will. All along, I knew what was right but my sinful nature wanted what was wrong, leaving me praying many days for the desire to change and today I'm transformed.

MY STRUGGLES

"THE FIGHT WAS WORTH IT"

 *The Fight Was Worth It*

Family Ties and Generational Curses

I come from a family where many of my relatives battled with a spirit of jealousy. It had gotten so bad for one of my uncles that it cost him his life. My uncle was always a victim of jealousy some way or another. He envied everything, mostly the women he dated. He would beat his women "to prove that he was a man" and "to keep them in line."

One day while my uncle was beating his girlfriend, she decided she was not going to continue being his punching bag. She grabbed the largest knife from the kitchen counter and told him with a stern voice, "Don't hit me again!" He punched her again knocking her to the floor. He got on top of her about to land another punch, but instead, she injected his heart with death. She remained on the floor in shock. My uncle stood up, and while stumbling like a drunk, he yelled "I'm a man" and snatched the knife from his chest. While the blood from his chest painted the kitchen floor he became weaker and weaker. But determined to finish what he started he got back on top of her and swung again, but this time his fist rested against her face, then he smiled and said, "You got me," and he rolled off her. By the time the ambulance made it there, he was added to the list of fatal attractions.

The Fight Was Worth It

Jealousy was not the only thing that crippled our family relationships. Witchcraft was another one. I would often hear family members discussing how other family member would cast spells causing illness or death. And if my family was not trying to cast spells, they thought they had become a victim of another warlock's spell.

The family that my parents, my brother, and I happen to be a part of is a family that does not bring me pride. Outside of the jealousy and witchcraft, my family spent their time getting high, drinking, partying, stealing, going in and out of jail, and fighting. Those same family members were the ones who could not keep a decent job. Many of my family members were from broken homes while others had no home at all. The single men would bring in various women, while some of the married men would either commit adultery, or allegedly dealt with homosexuality. The women in my family dealt with homosexuality, abuse, and promiscuity. Single parenting was also something that many members in my family were an article of.

At the same time or meanwhile, my parents were determined to raise us differently, while trying to stay connected with the family that we were outsiders too. My brother and I were raised with both parents, and we knew without a doubt, that we were loved by them. Our parents worked very hard to keep a roof over our heads, and they made every decision together. It was like we were living a perfect life but there was one thing that was missing, Sunday worship. My Dad and Mom always told us about

 *The Fight Was Worth It*

God's goodness, power, and love, but going to church was not a part of our routine.

People in our family thought we had everything. No one was thinking about the fact that we did not have a personal relationship with Christ. I don't know what it was about us, but it was like our family was trying to make our lives as much of a living Hell as they possibly could. My parents tried to ignore the fact that the only time our relatives would call was when they wanted something. We were stuck in a world where they did not want to involve us.

 *The Fight Was Worth It*

Really Auntie

My family was more worried about tearing us down instead of building us up. My parents, my brother, and I were criticized and rejected by relatives often. For everything that was positive in our lives they could find the negative. They were such bitter people. There was one family member in particular who tried to speak a curse over my life. This family member said that I would never amount to or have anything. She mentioned that I was going to be a high school dropout and never attend college. She said, "You will be rejected and disliked for the rest of your life."

She even spread lies about me and no one wanted to be around me. She claimed that I would never get married. She thought I would start having sex at an early age. She professed by fifteen I would have my first baby and continue having babies and sex with different guys.

"Today I am proud to say I have a number of children with the only guy that I have ever had intercourse with. I got kicked out of school but I'm in college. As of May 2012 I'm a college graduate."

Not only did my aunt think I would never be anything, but apparently my uncle thought the same thing. Although they were speaking death over my success, my mom was speaking success in my life. My mom would tell me, "KeeKee I believe in you. You will graduate, get

 *The Fight Was Worth It*

married, and be blessed with a wonderful family. KeeKee you are going to be blessed beyond measure."

My mom still believed my life would go the way she desired, even after my aunt spoke those horrible things over it. I was torn between the truth and a lie. I was hurt, not understanding why my family hated me, and spoke harsh lies about me. The sad part is that, they could lie about everything else, but they could not lie and say they loved us.

 *The Fight Was Worth It*

Grandfather Cold as Ice

My grandfather, my mother's dad, was cold toward me and my brother. He babysat my brother and me a few times while my parents worked, but I don't remember him feeding us. I don't remember him ever hugging us or saying hello, laughing with us, and I most certainly don't remember him ever saying he loved us. The only sound we would get from Grandpa was a grunt. I thought it was only fair to say maybe that was his personality, until we noticed the affection he showed toward the other grandchildren.

Even during Christmas he always got them something, but never got us anything. His reason was always "I forgot." I would be thinking, 'For the fourth Christmas in a row, yeah right.' I used to think he was only babysitting us to emotionally torture us. I remember the first time he conversed with us. My brother and I were watching videos and my grandfather walked to the front door after getting off the phone. On his way back past us he said, "Y'all daddy gone be late cause y'all Momma got stabbed or something like that, and she in the hospital."

I then asked, "So is she okay?"

And he told me, "I don't know, I didn't care to ask."

 *The Fight Was Worth It*

So my brother started crying saying, "I want Mom." My cold grandfather told him, "Shut up boy! If I knew you was gone cry, I wouldn't told you."

Shocked and emotionally bruised, what we had assumed for so long had now been revealed. I thought to myself, 'He really does hate mom, and he hates us too.'

I looked at my brother and he looked back at me with tears in his eyes. So, I grabbed my brother and embraced him. All we had at that moment was each other. I rocked with my brother and told him that it would be okay. From time to time, I would hear a car, so I would run and look out the window, but there was no sign of my parents. Then, I would go back to my brother and tell him, "Bro Bro that wasn't them, but they'll be here, we'll be alright."

My brother would look at me with his puppy dog eyes and say, "Okay KeeKee."

He then put his head back on my shoulder and continued to cry. Once my parents got there, all I saw was my mom's shirt ripped and covered in blood the same way I saw in a vision some days earlier. We got in the car and went to Zips, but I never said a word to my mom about what my grandpa said.

There was another time were he showed how cold he was. We were over to his house and he was naming his grandchildren to a friend of his. He named them all except for my brother and me. When my mom mentioned it to him he said, "Oh yeah them."

Then he repeated the names again leaving us out.

 *The Fight Was Worth It*

All I Have Is Mom, Dad, and Fes

Incidents like those caused in me a daily fear of losing my parents. Only God knows the drastic turn my life would have taken. I tried to move on, but I kept getting paralyzed by rejection and guilt. I thought it was my fault that I had uncles, aunts, cousins and grandparents that treated me as if I did not exist.

 *The Fight Was Worth It*

The Door of Rejection

Once I was old enough, I started to believe that my parents were lying to me about this caring and loving God. My parents would always tell me that God is love and wanted everybody to love one another. But God seemed not to be working this love hate relationship out for me and my family. This God that wanted everyone to love one another was not allowing me to receive anything but hate. He was like the hospital to me. I would go to Him for help, sometimes He would help and other times it seemed as though He couldn't. I was thinking, 'God is so unfair, does He understand this hurt that I'm enduring?'

Rejection opened the doors of my mind to tormenting demons. Often I could hear the enemy telling me I was not good enough, pretty enough, smart enough, or worthy enough to be a part of this thing called life. Whatever I felt I could do, the devil told me I couldn't. Daily I was in a fight with what I wanted, verses what the devil said I could not have. Whenever I would get the courage to go on, the devil would give me a gut busting insult by telling me, "You must be out your mind to think you can accomplish anything. You are a failure!"

I was then swallowed by insecurities and low self-esteem. For a very long time I believed everything the devil told me. I dealt with rejection and battles that caused my dreams to melt like a lit candle.

 *The Fight Was Worth It*

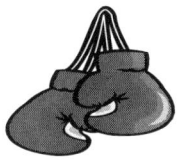

Darkness Swallow

Drowning in my own sorrow,
Swimming in a pool of emptiness,

Choking off my own vomit,
Hollow because of emptiness,

Mind being penetrated with ridiculousness,
Hallucinating from lies I was injected with
About to lose my grip of everything
Because nothing seems worth it.

Afflictions came to destroy me
But I was overcome by the great I am.

Joy unspeakable joy,
Peace that surpasses all understanding,

I am who I have become
Even though darkness tried to swallow me.

 *The Fight Was Worth It*

We Cry Together

With all the rejection from my family, my mom still tried to hold things together for me, taking on many titles. She was my mother, grandparents, sister, best friend; my teacher, doctor, lawyer, counselor; my banker, dictionary, comedian and my hero. I had everything that I could ever need or want in my mom, but I still found myself very unhappy. My mom noticed that I was hurting so she tried to fill my void. She tried to replace the void with love, cash, clothes, and cars.

    I got my first car when I was fifteen years old but I was still unhappy. Once I started working, my mom would let me put my checks in the bank, while she paid for everything to help me build my bank account, but I was still unhappy. My mom did not have a lot of money, but she was willing to go lacking just to make sure I had what I needed.

    With all that I had, I never felt I had enough. I use to pray to God for more wealth, happiness, and help but nothing seemed to change. I seemed to have been bitten by the unfortunate bug. My mom would try to fix every problem but she quickly realized that she was my mom, not a miracle worker. Whenever she saw that I was hurting she would cry with me. Meanwhile at school, I was dealing with a whole other ball game and they were hurting every bit of my character.

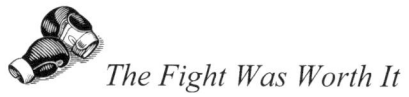 *The Fight Was Worth It*

A Different Kind of Lesson

In school I was set apart, under indulged by life because I was a misfit. I was hated by many and loved by a few. Therefore I had more enemies than friends. I was starting to see the curse that my aunt spoke over my life being handed over to me like a baby to his mother after delivery.

People knew I was different as I sat in the corner, too afraid to speak, yet hoping to be accepted. There were also times I would take a risk and act like a buffoon. But that made things worse. It seemed like the chances of me being accepted was like winning the lottery. My differences made way for me to be the punch line to many jokes, the outcast in every bunch, and the loner with no friends.

In school I got picked on a lot. There were times where spit would be dripping from my face like sweat, because somebody decided to make me their spitting target as I walked the halls. I was not tough enough to handle my problems at school, so I would take it out on my parents. Other times, people would rant calling me all types of names, including 'weirdo' and 'freak.' I was labeled a 'freak,' although I was not having intercourse of any kind or performing oral sex.

Not only were the students calling me names, but the teachers were too. The teachers labeled me as stupid, so they had given up on me. Yeah, I must admit, I was a

 *The Fight Was Worth It*

problem child with a G.P.A of 0.6, but what does a middle school or high school student do when it seems as though more than half of the school is against them?

Every day seemed harder than the day before, but the hardest time for me was lunchtime. During lunchtime students would take my food and eat it, they would throw it at me, or trash it. I was out numbered, so I was too afraid to fight back. I would eat in the restroom stalls hiding, sitting on the toilets, hoping that no one would see me. However, there was a time when I got caught and I lied and said I was using the restroom.

Too embarrassed to continue eating in the restroom, there were many days I would not eat at all. People had now pushed me to the breaking point. The actions of my family, peers, and teachers caused me to hate just about everybody. With this foundation of hatred came distrust towards everybody except for my parents and my brother. I was tired of all this humiliation. I now wanted to do something to get back at those who'd hurt me without a cause. I was done praying. What was the point in continuing to pray when things were not getting any better?

 *The Fight Was Worth It*

PSALMS 13: 1-4 (NLT)

O Lord, how long will you forget me? Forever?

How long will you look the other way?

How long must I struggle with anguish in my soul,

with sorrow in my heart every day? How long will my

enemy have the upper hand? Turn and answer me, O Lord

my God! Restore the sparkle to my eyes, or I will die.

Don't let my enemies gloat, saying, "We have defeated

her!" Don't let them rejoice at my downfall.

 *The Fight Was Worth It*

Satan Here I Come

I felt like I was at the edge of death and one wrong move could have ended it all. Frustrated, because I was tired of being ridiculed, I decided to take on something that changed the course of my life. I was at a point where I experienced a homicidal break down. I killed who I was to practice Satanism.

I started to dabble with witchcraft as I intimately worshipped Satan. I was playing a deadly game with God and the grim reaper was going to be my prize. I was worshipping Satan not knowing that I was really being insulted by the enemy's antics. The devil comes to steal, kill, and destroy, and he had destroyed almost every piece of me. He was using people from every back ground to harvest a raging anger within me.

Before I gave my life away, I was timorous when it came to just the thought of harming someone. After I converted to Satanism, just the thought of hurting or killing someone was therapeutic. My mind would have an orgasm at every thought of harm or death. Not only did the thoughts feel good, but it was like tickling a baby. I was laughing but yet, I was hurting. Angry, I was no longer conscious of what was right. My family had a history with witchcraft so I already felt like I was a pro. I watched movies that dealt with this so I knew just where to start. I had voodoo dolls, pins with the colorful tips to stick the dolls with, and an Ouija board. I would be in my room

 *The Fight Was Worth It*

trying to cast spells, plotting to kill those that hurt me, seeking answers from the devil, and hoping to conjure the dead. There were days I would cast a spell on someone and the next day that person would not come to school. I'm not sure if the witchcraft worked or not, but if it did, I felt like the curse was vindicated "at that time."

 *The Fight Was Worth It*

Wear Me Out

Now that I was one with darkness, my entire wardrobe changed. I wore black lipstick, black nail polish, I kept my hair jet black; and I wore black or dark clothing; but people still didn't understand what I had done. Once I became one with the enemy it was like my eyes were opened because I saw things in a new way. I was no longer a puppet being controlled by humiliation. My anger and hatred towards people had bubbled over like boiling water on a stove. I was tired of what I was going through so I felt like I had no choice but to worship Satan. I now felt privileged by what I called a blessing from the enemy, but really I was cursed.

The enemy caught me when I was wrapped up in my feelings so he tricked me into eliminating God as my source.

The devil didn't leave much room for me to believe on God, because he would always confirm why I stopped believing in the first place. "If there is a God that is so caring and kind, where was He when these kids were picking on you, making fun of you, and spreading lies about you? If there is a God, where is He when people get hurt, sick, or die? When your mom was attacked and all you saw was her covered in blood, where was this God? When you are crying at night because you are tired of being sick and tired, where is God? You prayed for God to stop

 *The Fight Was Worth It*

and kill those people that picked on you, instead things got worse, so where is God?"

The questions the devil asked me made sense causing more anger, so I denied God. I could no longer call on the name of Jesus, and if I did, I would ask God to forgive me. I could not look at anything that represented holiness, and if I did, it would burn my eyes. For me to hear anything about Jesus was like nails to a chalkboard, or poison to my belly. Anytime I would hear about Christ I would have a terroristic anger. I no longer cared what God wanted or who He was. I made up my mind that I would never trust God again. All I could say in my heart was, 'God if you are real, where are you?'

 *The Fight Was Worth It*

Unworthy

I was now swimming in bitterness and about to drown in the lake of fire if I didn't soon change. I didn't care about dying because I didn't see the point in living. I was angry at God so I took an interest in what was Satanic. Now that I was worshipping Satan I felt invisible. My fears were now in hibernation while everything else was elevated.

I dealt with an increasing battle of low self-esteem, attempts of suicide, homosexuality, addictions and alcoholism. I dealt with depression, a murderous spirit, and the fear of getting caught before I finished every murder that I had planned. Then there was disobedience, failing at everything, anger, and hatred. Daily I would try to redefine myself, because I did not know who I was anymore. Those were some, but not all of my daily tormenting battles that attached themselves to me after I decided to worship Satan. I would look in the mirror, but could not recognize my own face. I had become a monster. The innocent girl that I used to be was no longer there.

I would inflict pain on myself because the devil tricked me into believing that pain brought pleasure. I did drugs and alcohol on a regular to forget about my problems. My life had gotten so bad at times, that I could not function without an illegal substance in my system. Once the high was gone the problems came back. I was

 *The Fight Was Worth It*

desperate, so I started cooking up coke because marijuana was not doing it anymore, and the baking soda had no affects either. I chewed tobacco, sniffed glue, inhaled empty spray paint cans, and I loved the smell of gasoline for a quick buzz. I made myself into a fiend.

I was on a flight to Hell with my master, Satan. Satan was the pilot on this flight and my life was about to erupt into eternal damnation if I did not accept Christ as my personal Lord and Savior soon. However, at the time Christ and accepting Him were the furthest things from my mind.

 *The Fight Was Worth It*

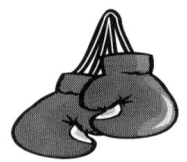

The Devil Almost Had Me

Many have the story of abuse
But mine is different

Many have the story of shame
But mine is different

I am a walking, talking, fighting testimony
I am a vigorous, victorious, AND virtuous woman

I used to be where the devil had me
And I was so caught up in that lifestyle
That I didn't know how to be free

As the devil tortured my mind, soul, and body

The devil used to get all in my head
Telling me I would be better off dead
At the time I didn't know the Word of God
So, I was eating up the lies that I
Was being fed

The devil used to talk to my mind
About a life of crime
Telling me how I could be respected
If I "got on my grind"

 *The Fight Was Worth It*

He would tell me what I wanted to hear
As he made love to my mind
Making me feel good
As he filled my head with lies…

I was so weak
And vulnerable to his voice
So anger was my mentality
Because the enemy was my Lord

The enemy kept pushing me
Which kept me on edge
It was just a matter of time
Before I would snap and
Shhhhh
I'll keep that silent instead…

I started to fear what I might do
Because I lost my sanity

Not that I was crazy
But because I was listening to the enemy

The moment the enemy manipulated my mind
I was screwed
And there after I started believing
There was no God to save me
But in all fairness I was just a fool…

I put on this persona
So when people saw me they saw hate

So nobody wanted to be around me
And to be honest at times it wasn't safe

The Fight Was Worth It

I couldn't love anybody
I didn't know how to love myself…

I was just ready to lay hands on people
And those were hands of death…

I started hating myself
And I must admit
The more I would listen to the enemy
Of life I became tired of it

I started to torture myself
Because that was the next thing to do

The enemy already had my mind
So it was easier for my body
To become his temple too
Because I thought I had nothing to lose

 *The Fight Was Worth It*

Death Wish

I was now skipping school more often, because everything besides death seemed pointless. My ire towards life had me trying to cut and burn my pain away. Other times I would be contemplating suicide almost at every thought. I had become fond of the suicide journey that I was trying to embark. I was starving for death. I tried catering myself different dishes of death, but each one left my stomach growling for more.

One of my death appetites called for a knife, a plate of intestines, and a cup of blood. I remember taking a kitchen knife and jabbing it into my stomach hoping to reach my intestines. The first time I jabbed the knife into my stomach it bounced back. The second time I jabbed the knife into my stomach my mom came into the room and broke my concentration. The knife bounced back, and it hurt so badly. I made sure that would be my last time trying that method of what I called, '*Death on a Plate.*' I pierced my skin, but it left me with more pain than pleasure.

Another time I tried my hand at suicide was the deadly technique that I called, '*Is My Killing in Vein?*' I remember taking a knife to my vein and slicing from east to west. I was hoping that the blood from my wrist would flow like a raging river. But instead I watched the blood drip from my wrist like a dripping faucet. I soon realized this attempt was not going to be enough to put me out of my misery. Then, my parents knocked on the restroom door so that plan was spoiled too.

The Fight Was Worth It

After so many painful failed attempts at suicide, I decided to take a less painful approach. I tried pills and alcohol at the same time hoping to sleep to death. I call this one, *'Sleeping Beautifully.'* I remember taking about seven Tylenol pills and drinking a 24oz can of beer. I wrote my parents a note telling them that my death was from suicide and not natural causes, than I closed my eyes. I slept better than I slept in a long time. The next day I woke up using every profane word I could think of because I was still here.

Then I started thinking, 'Maybe I could drive myself to death.' I call this one, *'Driving Ms. Crazy.'* I started running red lights and stop signs at any given moment trying to take myself out, and I did not care who went with me. I had a death wish, but instead of dying, I got lots of tickets. Nothing seemed to work so far, so I was about to try my final attempt at death.

This one is called *'She Got Brain.'* I tried getting angry at everybody hoping someone would blow my brain out, but again, I was unsuccessful. So one day I thought, 'Once I get home, I just have to do it myself.'

Once I got home I grabbed a gun and went into the basement. It felt like I was walking through a tunnel, and at the end of the tunnel was death. The power was now in my hands and I was ready to let my brain meet the basement wall. I call this one, *"The Eye of The Revolver."* I sat on the basement floor with my back against the wall. For so long it had been the world against me, but this time it was going to be the gun against my face. I was caressing the gun with one hand and using the other hand for my joint. Once I

 *The Fight Was Worth It*

finished my last, of several joints, I fired up a black and mild. As I formed smoke circles with my mouth and watched it vanish. I knew my life was going to soon be like that smoke circle. My life was already a circle of failure, rejection, and pain. Now all I needed was my life to disappear.

At this point my smile was completely gone and happiness was just a glimpse of my imagination. I hungered after death. I was a walking suicidal time bomb. I was living but the devil tricked me into believing that my life had no purpose.

So, after I finished my black and mild, I kissed the gun, and went into a deep trance. I saw myself playing Russian roulette. I pulled the trigger back and all I heard was click, click, bang! I then felt the warmth of the blood rolling down my face. My eyes were eventually cloudy from the blood which was going to stain them. I did not feel a thing, but I could taste the salt in my mouth. I did not know what happened or who did it, but I saw it. I saw myself dying, then I felt myself choking, that's when I realized it was just a vision. The vision of me seeing myself bleeding to death was my reality check. I realized I was not as cold blooded as I thought I was. I realized I did not hate myself as much as I thought I did. So I tucked the gun away in my pants. I called my brother down stairs to make him an accessory to my murder. "Fes!"

He came running down the stairs. "Yeah."

"Bro Bro, I need a big favor."

The Fight Was Worth It

"What? Anything for you KeeKee."

So I pulled the gun out and he jumped back like he was playing double dug.

"Woe, what you doing with that?"

"I want you to use it to blow my brains out."

He giggled a little. "What!... Why?" He asked with the smile still on his face.

"I'm just tired of life."

"Me too KeeKee, I want to kill myself too sometimes, but I don't try doing it."

"Okay I tell you what, we can do it together."

"How KeeKee, we only got one gun?"

I was not expecting my death to be this difficult. He was a young buck, but he was asking wise questions. I had to keep my cool because I didn't want him to panic and leave me all alone with no one to pull the trigger.

"Well Bro Bro I tell you what, shoot me first; here." I handed him the gun. " There's the gun, now shoot me, close your eyes."

So with the gun in his hand, he put it right up to my face. He closed his eyes then I closed mine. I was thinking, 'Man he is about to do it? He is one cold blooded joker.' But, I could not let him see me sweat under pressure so I asked,

 *The Fight Was Worth It*

"Are you ready, are you sure you want to do this?"

"No."

"Well Bro Bro you said anything I wanted."

"Well yeah, that was before I knew what it was."

So that's when he put the gun down. I was thinking, 'Dang my stupid self just talked my brother out of killing me.' So, I now had to find a way to redirect my brother's mind back into killing mode.

"Well Bro Bro, if you don't do it, I won't be your friend anymore."

"And if I do it, you still won't be my friend because you'll be dead KeeKee."

"You right, so what we gone do?" He was blowing my high, all my plans were dropping like dead flies, and I was all out of plan, until he said,

"Okay I will do it, but if I shoot you, who will shoot me?"

"I will."

"But you will be dead KeeKee."

"I will shoot you before I die."

"I don't know about that KeeKee."

 *The Fight Was Worth It*

"Fes just hurry up and do it, stop asking questions and shoot!" So, I grabbed the gun and pointed it towards him with my finger on the trigger.

He took two steps back. "What KeeKee?" He stretched his arms out the same way Jesus stretched His on the cross and said, "So you gone kill me?"

"KeeKee, Fes, I'm home come here!"

We both looked at each other and yelled, "Daddy!" Leaving the revolver on the pool table, we ran upstairs before we were involved in a murder-suicide. Once again I was stopped before I accomplished my mission for death. I was now more depressed than ever. The devil was supposed to take the place of God to make my life better, but instead he was tormenting me death.

 *The Fight Was Worth It*

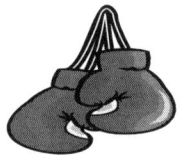

Dear God,

Lord, I'm searching because I hoped to find my purpose

Lost in a world that does not display anything worth searching for

Ignoring the fact that your death was the purpose worth living for

Hiding from you because at times I feel you don't care. Other times I feel you have delayed coming through for me.
Lord, I am searching for purpose because I'm missing you.
Lord, I'm thirsty and confused not sure of what to do.

I feared what others may think of me while I was caring less about you.

I was slothful
And I was empty of zeal
So I was quiet because I wasn't sure you were real.

 *The Fight Was Worth It*

God Will Prove Himself

I really thought I could make it throughout life without Christ guiding me. I was seeking death not realizing that I was already dead without Christ being my life support. There were many days God tried to prove Himself to me, and while He was trying to prove Himself, I was continuing to doubt that He existed at all. In whatever way I could disrespect or doubt God I would. I remember doubting God one time while in the car with my parents and my parents said God will prove himself and I said, "Yeah right, okay."

My eight year old cousin was lying on the door, when my dad turned the corner, the door swung open, no seat belt, but my cousin did not fall out. This happened not once, not twice, but three times in a row after I doubted God's existence. My mom didn't say much but my dad yelled out, "I told you He'll prove Himself!"

My reply was, and I may have laughed, "It probably was a coincidence."

I believe my mom knew what was ahead for me because she told me something that I would never forget.

"KeeKee, if you don't hurry up and change your ways, I'm afraid that you will end up dying prematurely, and it will hurt us like hell."

The Fight Was Worth It

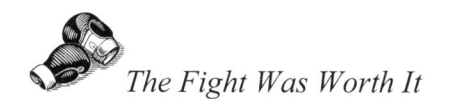

Missionaries Witnessing

Not really sure what just happened with my cousin, and tripping off what my mom just told me, my mind was wondering. Before I went to bed that night my parents let me know they loved me and were praying for me. As the nights turned days, I was going to soon experience what I've been waiting for. The word tells us there is always warning before destruction. I was warned, but God loved me enough to warn me again, and then destruction.

For the next few weeks everywhere I went someone was told me about God. Different people would tell me that God cares for me and that he loves me, but I didn't want to listen. These strangers were saying the same things that Mom and Dad had said. I started thinking; 'Maybe there is a God that loves me, but until I find out, I'm gonna keep doing me.'

The Fight Was Worth It

Crazy High, Was My Blunt Laced

On October 5, I met this guy at the dollar show. He and I seemed to have a connection right away. He thought he knew me and I thought I knew him but we had never met before. He said that he wanted to kick it with me. At first I was skeptical then I got to thinking; 'My parents really don't let me do much. I've never been out, had a boyfriend. I never attended a homecoming or prom. Up to this point, I never did much of anything that I wanted to do because Mom and Dad are so protective of me. They are always trying to control me. This could be my opportunity to have sex for the first time, just to prove a point to them. In a way, I could get Mom and Dad back for keeping me hostage in the house. Naw, I don't want to have sex with him, but if he raped me that would be up my alley. I want to get raped anyway so I could play the helpless victim. That would be so sexy if he would beat me while we had sex. I feel like if we have sex, he will fall in love with me. I don't think it would be like Mom and Dad said. I don't think he will leave me after we have sex. That's just another way of them tricking me into doing what they wanted me to do, waiting until marriage. Please!'

So, that day we set up a date for October 7. I did not know this young man any more than I knew a painter by his painting, but I knew it was going to be "on and popping."

The Fight Was Worth It

Normally, I would not trust anyone, but I was tired of my parents trying to control me, so I was doing "me" that day.

So on October 7 we agreed that I would skip school. At first I was going to take my car but I heard a voice tell me not to (even in our mess God speaks to us.) So, we met just like we planned. I dropped my car off at school and we headed to Northland Mall to get high.

On our way to Northland Mall, I happened to see my brother. When we stopped for him, he said he didn't know what he was doing but he wanted to make sure I was alright. It didn't make sense at the time, but I told him I was cool and offered him to ride along with me and this guy that I did not know. I did not know that I was minutes away from a near death experience. Once we pulled up to the mall and parked, he pulled out the Philly blunt. It was like I could hear the paper crackling as he sliced it. He emptied the Philly blunt then pulled out the dime bag and spread the green onto the blunt like someone was laying lettuce on a burger. He gave me the honors of licking and sealing it.

As he was using the cigarette lighter to dry the blunt he was staring at me with a weird look in his face. I was thinking, 'Okay this dude is about to kill me in front of my brother. It's all my fault too, because my stupid self dragged my brother into this.'

Then the dude said something that had me really thinking I was about to die. He said, "Man the stuff I would do to you if your brother was not here."

The Fight Was Worth It

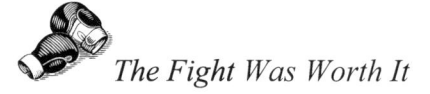

So I asked him, "Like what? You can tell me."

"Nothing. You probably won't be able to handle it anyway. How many dudes you let hit that?"

"None. I'm still a virgin."

"A virgin? You lying. I don't know no girls your age that's a virgin."

"I am though."

"Yeah, you wouldn't be able to handle this."

I know I should have run at that point, but I was not about to miss out on my daily high. Plus, my brother was there so what was he going to do to me? So the dude asked me, "Have you ever got high before?"

"Yeah, I told you I get high all the time."

"Yeah, but that stuff you had probably was that doo doo. This stuff here is the real deal."

I hardly had the slightest idea what he really meant by "real deal", but I told him, "Yeah the stuff that I get be that real deal too."

And he told me, "Okay we'll see."

I told him, "Yes we will see, I can handle anything. If we had sex I'll be able to handle that too." I then started thinking, 'Why did I just say that? This dude is about to kill me and drive my body to some remote place where my parents will never find me, then he gone rape me.'

The Fight Was Worth It

He told me to take the first puff because he could tell if I smoked weed before based on how I puff it. So, once I puffed he yelled, "You is a amateur Cuzz!" And he started laughing.

"No I aint. I do this all the time!" I was about to prove to this guy that I was not an amateur weed smoker. So, with the blunt in between my fingers, I licked my lips. I was thinking, 'This can't be too much different than smoking a Jay.' I put the blunt in between my lips. I inhaled, filling my little lungs with as much smoke as I could. Once my lungs were completely filled I swallowed and started choking.

I saw dark smoke swimming into the air like hot air balloon being released. Everything instantly started to look the way it looks on a movie when a person is in dream mode. I instantly started hallucinating while going crazy at the same time. I looked at my brother and he was laughing at me but I didn't know why. I asked him, "What you laughing at? I got doo doo on my face or something Bro Bro?"

I looked at the dude and he was laughing too. So I said, "What Cuzz, you see these ants crawling on my face?"

Then my brother started calling me at the same time the dude was telling me I was tripping. It sounded like they were talking through an intercom. The dude asked me, "Are you cool?"

"Yeah, I just got to get these ants off me, Cuzz."

The Fight Was Worth It

"Ants, what ants?"

"These ants that's crawling on me." I know at that point I had to be looking like a geekier. I then started to hear my heart beating. "A cuzz my heart is beating."

"It is supposed to beat. Man have your sister got high before?"

"Yeah, we get high every day after school."

"Naw my heart ain't supposed to beat. This is the first time my heart has ever beat in my life. I must be dying."

"No you ain't dying. You'd be dead if it wasn't beating."

I started laughing and told them, "Y'all trippen."

At that point, I started burning and I still felt ants crawling all over me. I was sitting in the front on the passenger side rocking back and forth like a crack head desperate for another pipe. I became a stripper and started pulling my clothes off. I was pulling my clothes off because it felt like the ants had been dipped in gasoline and my skin was the flame.

I hopped out of the car because I thought I was on fire. There was this car driving down the parking lot that I felt it would be fun to chase. I jumped in front of the car and he slammed on his brakes then rested on his horn. His horn sounded similar to a blow horn to me, causing me to literally almost crap my pants.

The Fight Was Worth It

Then, I spotted these two people that were coming out of the store. I got down on all fours and started chasing behind them barking like a dog. Then, I started licking my arm. I was blurting out profane things to cars and people as they drove and walked down the parking lot. Other times I was throwing stuff at cars. I remember dancing in the middle of the parking lot. I was just doing whatever my mind told me to do. I knew what I was doing. I just had no way of controlling it. The dude was yelling from the car, "Get in the car before you get locked up!"

I yelled back, "Forget the police! They don't want none of this!" And I did a sexual dance.

"Get in the car now! You are supposed to be at school anyway! I knew this was a bad idea! Come on please! Let me just take you home!"

"Well my car is at school so I ain't going nowhere."

"Okay, get in the car and I will take you to school to get your car! Just please get in the car!"

So, I got in the car and he took me straight to school. I could smell the sweat from his body as he was perspiring from fear. Once we made it to school my brother took my car keys. I yelled out, "You better not hurt my (blank blank) brother!"

The dude then got out of the car and started walking towards me. He grabbed me and said. "Any other dude would have taken advantage of you. Just go to the office. I got to go."

The Fight Was Worth It

"What time is it?"

"I got…just go to class. Just go to the office so they can call someone to pick you up. Don't mention my name for nothing."

"I love you and I won't hurt you guy." Once I got into the building I went straight to class, and I made an entrance. I took the chalk out the teacher's hand and threw it. The teacher said if I do it again I would be in trouble. I apologized and sat down. I raised my hand and said, "Teacher why do I got all these holes in my skin? That is probably why I keep itching."

The laughter of teenagers rumbled the room.

"That's it Keelanashe', get out of my classroom and go to the office!"

She buzzed the office and let them know I was on my way. She also mentioned how she thought I may have been under the influence of something.

"A, teacher are you that fat? Oh I forgot. You is just pregnant."

So, as I made my way to the office I was feeling a combination of paranoia and toughness. I thought everybody wanted to fight me. I thought everybody was laughing at me. I interrupted every class that I passed. I walked up the stairs, stood there, and looked down.

I remember wondered how my spit would look once it smacked against the floor. Once I spit the first time, I was highly entertained watching it hit the floor three more times. I started wondering how the floor underneath me would look with my brain polished on it.

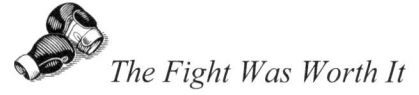

My problem was that I just could not figure out how to jump over the banister, or maybe I did not have enough strength to do so. So, I dragged myself back down the stairs. As I walked the halls I was so paranoid, it felt like everybody was staring at me. When I finally made it to the main office I blurted out, "What is everybody staring at?"

Once I made it to the Dean's office he told me. "I been waiting for you. I was just about to come get you myself."

"For what? You see I made it here by myself. I don't want to be seen with no bald headed old man."

He asked me what was going on because that behavior was not normal for me. I kept telling him everything was wrong. I told him I was ready to go home and I started crying, then laughing, then crying again I was messed up.

But instead he said he was calling the ambulance because I needed to go to the hospital. Out of anger I knocked everything off the walls in his office and pushed everything off his desk. He asked me to sign something and I spit on it and cursed at him. Once the paramedics got there I remember my heart was beating so hard and loud that I could see it pumping outside of my shirt. I remember getting put on the stretcher, being strapped in, hearing the sirens and then I blacked out.

The Fight Was Worth It

Death Becomes Me

I was in and out of consciousness and on the verge of death. I had smoked something that caused my life to be slowly drifting away. While the doctors worked to stabilize me, I started to hallucinate about my parents. My parents were telling me about Christ and if I accepted Him I would live. I did not want to hear that, I was ready to die.

As I lie there, lifeless, I could hear and see the doctors but I could not move or speak. I could feel my lifeless body going through withdrawals. I was experiencing death. At that moment I realized I was not as ready to die as I thought I was, but my pride would not let me humble myself. I heard a voice telling me to call on Jesus. I said, "I rather die than call on the name of the Lord!"

At that moment, the vision of my parents vanished like clearing smoke. I believe God used angels that looked like them in order to reach me. I then heard another voice say, "If you die now you would go straight to Hell."

One day my parents told me, "Even if it's on your dying bed, you will call on the name of the Lord".

I remember thinking, 'Wow could this be it?'

The Fight Was Worth It

Leaving Without Saying Good Bye

At that moment my life and everything I was taught about Christ flashed right before my eyes like lightning. I had to call on Christ or die. I called on Christ in my heart and asked Him to forgive me. We serve such a mighty and forgiving God.

Before that day there were many days I would disrespect God to try and prove that He did not exist. If he did exist, I was trying to prove that He was powerless. Although I was disrespectful to Him for many years, the day I asked for forgiveness God heard me and forgave me. Not only did He hear me, and forgive me, but He no longer held me to my past.

I thought I was in control of my life but really I was being controlled by Satan. The one that I looked up to for so long was the one that wanted me dead. It was the one that I rejected that thought enough of me to give me life. Jesus snatched me from the claws of death, and my lifeless body now had life. I heard one doctor exclaim, "It's a miracle!"

Then he started speaking using medical terminology. However, I was able to understand when he said that I was closer to death than the two girls that they lost earlier that day.

The Fight Was Worth It

I was extremely drained but I was now able to move and speak. My first word was Jesus. I had finally called on the name of Jesus. I opened my mouth and I could not stop calling His name and thanking Him. That situation changed me. Now the door of Satanism for me was shut, and the door to my heart concerning Christ was opened. At that point I realized even though I doubted God many days, there was a part of me that knew He was real. But being that I was an extremely prideful person I was willing to let pride take me to my grave. That was another near death experience, but I survived, and I realized that my life really does have a purpose.

The Fight Was Worth It

'Pain In My Eyes'

I am a survivor!

I've been through the storm of despair, depression
And attempts of suicide

I've been through the storm of abuse of every kind

I've been through the storm of neglect, heartbreak and pain
What I've been through was almost unto death
But I survived

I could not be more ready to share my story than I am now
Look

I stared death right in the eyes
But I survived

I jumped on the bull of death
But was held on by life
And yet I survived another day

I was caressing the gun while it was at my own face
But I survived

It was a stimulating feeling because I was so at will
to die…

I could feel the adrenaline rush as life as I knew it

The Fight Was Worth It

Would pass me by
And be no more…

The very life that I
For years was trying to escape
Was finally going to end but

I knew my life was not going to end
By some man's hands around my throat

I knew my life was going to end
But
I knew it was not going to end by me overdosing on coke

I was just ready to say bye bye to this presumptuous world
Because I've been bound too long
I've fought too hard
And I've cried my last tear…

The power was now in my hands
And I was ready to go to my home away from home
So I was gripping this ice coldness to steal, kill, and destroy
my own soul
I was ready to vanish and leave my body behind to suffer
no more

But I was not going to die by a man,
I was going to kill…
myself…

My very motives were evil, toward me
My heartbeat was a murmur
Which I hoped would cause my death,
Then I would gain the victory
Because I was unhappy with life
I did not understand being a wife

The Fight Was Worth It

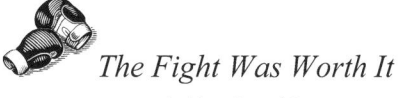

I was full of strife
And all I could think about was death…

I was running a race but no one was running but me
I was repulsive to the saying I could be all I could be
I was not at liberty to live at my best
Because I,
I was my own enemy
Because I didn't realize my life was just a testimony

I vowed that I could not change
But was it that I would not change
Because I feared I would always be the same

Even when others saw me at my best,
I would put my worst foot forward to end up with my foot
In my chest…

Death for me was a daily game I played

Death and I were like Sylvester and Tweety Bird
I was after death
But it would always end up in the cage
So the closer I got to death
And how I didn't die was simply amazing

At that point I starting to think I was invisible,
The fact that I survived this long is incredible
Because the way I saw life
And the way I lived life was despicable

It was like
Nothing was getting better
And I didn't know why
I kept questioning God every time I would cry
But finally I heard a voice speak,

The Fight Was Worth It

'The Pain In My Eyes',
Which means,
Things are not the way they seem
It was a deception of lies,
A deception of lies that spiraled out of control
When I got comfortable with sin and only God knows
How deep my sin was…

I was full of sin
Full of pride
I couldn't confess my sins
So my sins I would hide

And when I had an opportunity to come clean
I would keep quiet and stayed glued to my seat
Hoping no one would notice me

But all along God was trying to get my attention
So he kept sending the missionaries to witness
They would tell me God loves me
And he has not forsaken me because he cares
And even though I seemed alone God was right there
And it was only because of God's grace and mercy…

That my life was spared…

Come to find out God had something in me
That I could not see
But the devil saw it
So he was using me to destroy me…

The devil was after me so hard
Because he saw that I was worthy…

I can now say it myself,

The Fight Was Worth It
I know that I am worthy …

Worthy of the ground that I stand on,
To stand against life's adversities
Because I am made in God's image

I am now at liberty to be the best I can be
Because I am a Reflection of Christ
And through Him He has made the impossible
Possible for me,

He has shown me through His Word that He died for me
And the moment I accepted Christ as my personal Savior
That moment made me impeccable

So the life that I lived prior to this day,
For me
Is no longer regrettable

And like my husband Will Roc says,
"It's these new shoes man, it's these new shoes!"
So, I'm not walking shameful about my past
This moment only made possible by my Heavenly Dad
Every moment that I breathe is now a Spiritual brag…

Because

If I didn't live my life, the way I lived it
I would not have a story
Glory be to God that we are overcome
By the words of our testimonies
Glory be to God!

The Fight Was Worth It

Death of a Teacher, or Not

One week later, I could still feel the effects of whatever my blunt was laced with that autumn day in October. Coming that close to death made me realize that I was not ready to die. That situation caused me to learn a little about humility. After going through all of that, I felt there was an urgency to consider what my parents been telling me about Christianity. Even though I felt the urgency, I didn't know how to change, so I sat there waiting for a sign.

While I sat there waiting for a sign, I was thinking about how much I've let my parents down. I was expelled on October 7th. I was hoping for the chance to take one more grab at my diploma because I knew how badly my mom wanted to see her first born walk the stage. Just when it seemed like all failed, Jennings offered an alternative program for students that were previously kicked out of school. Thrilled, I hopped on the opportunity, not knowing I was going to be degraded in this program as well.

Seemingly, there was a female that was kicked out of school for having sex. Since I was the only female in the program, rumor had it that the female was me. I responded to their rumors and told them, "There probably was a female that got kicked out for having sex, but it wasn't me."

I had to deal with that dispute for a while. I felt devastated. With all the pressure that was on me, I continued to do my best. I was no longer going to let my peers hinder my progress. I was there to get my diploma. I wanted my diploma as badly as a hungry baby wants his bottle.

The Fight Was Worth It

After a while the allegations of what's done in the dark came to light. There was a female that came to the program and showed true signs of freakiness to the ninth power. The students were now starting to believe the fact that my "pleasure box" did not receive stimulation at school. I was now being accepted by the students so things were headed uphill for me... until the day things went outrageously wrong.

The way the incident happened, seemed like a set up to get me kicked out of the program. At the end of the day we were leaving class and one of the students called one of the teachers' a female dog under her breath. I immediately started thinking, 'Man that was messed up. I wonder why she called the teacher a female dog. Oh well, as long as the teacher didn't hear her.' The next thing I know, the teacher was calling me back. Okay, I'm thinking, 'Maybe I forgot something.' To my surprise my teacher must have had ears like a dog because he heard her. He asked me, "What did you say as you were leaving the class?"

I told him, "Nothing, I just said bye."

"Keela I am going to give you one more chance. What did you say as you were leaving?"

"I said bye, that's it."

"What else did you say?"

"Nothing else."

"I heard you say bye, *b*."

"What! No, I said bye and someone else said the other word."

"Keela, I know your voice."

The Fight Was Worth It

I started laughing, because I was about to become a gymnast and flip.

"Dude! You got me mistaken. You need to get your ears checked."

"And you are still being disrespectful. "

He grabbed some paper then signed it and gave it to me.

"So what, you kicking me out the program?"

"You can't return to school until a meeting takes place. I will speak with your dean in the morning."

He then went on to pretty much tell me that they were not going to tolerate the disrespect from me. The program is for those looking for a second chance and those that want to do better. I was blown back like some hair in the wind when he suggested getting my G.E.D would be a better route for me.

I was distraught. I exited the building and it was as if my sanity left too. As I looked for my car keys I could feel my temples pounding like drums. I started my car and took off. My head was spinning like a merry go round as I drove down Jennings Station Rd at 70 miles per hour. I was in a zone. I started thinking, 'This is the ultimate betrayal. He betrayed me and I betrayed my mom. I will never be able to get my high school diploma. After all I put mom through this is going to hurt her, by far, the worst!' At that moment my mind was inverted and I thought, 'I can't let him get by with this. I am going to kill that dude!' Whenever I got upset my first instinct was murder.

That's when I noticed the red light, and a guy crossing the street. When I noticed the light and the man, I gripped the steering wheel as I felt my body draw back. I remember smashing on my brake and briefly losing control of my car. I

The Fight Was Worth It

remember my ears welcoming the screeching of my tires. My nose was accompanied by the smell of melted rubber. My eyes acknowledged the rubber from my tires going up like black confetti.

For a moment I was lost in a world of uncertainty. I was compromising between the truth and reality. The truth of the matter was that I got kicked out of school, but the reality was that it wasn't the end of the world for me. But it was the end of my belief in God, I felt like he failed me once again. With the desperation to kill, an innocent man's life was almost riddled by death.

When I got home that evening, I told my parents I wasn't feeling well so I was going to lie down. In my mind, sleep was going to make the night pass faster. Once my parents said they hoped I felt better, I was thinking, 'I will feel better as soon as I put dude to sleep. He stabbed me in my back and caused me to break my mom's heart. So, I am going to stab him in his back over thirty times then cut out his heart while I talk to him. While he is laying there helpless and bleeding to death, I am going to put his heart in the palm of his hand instead of an apple. That will make me feel better. I would have taught him to never ever do anyone else the way he did me.'

After much pondering I finally fell asleep. The next morning I was lost in thought again, not understanding why I was the black sheep of everything. Not understanding why people kept telling lies about me. I didn't understand why I lived, only to end up feeling like I would be better off dead. The more I thought on those things the more my anger would intensify. I was at a point where my parents were not going to be able to talk me out of this one.

So I played my role like a hand of cards. For every move that my parents made, I would make a move hoping they didn't

The Fight Was Worth It

see my hand. I had premeditated this murder so that it could be precise, but sharp, and I was going to leave with a clean slate. In my mind there was not going to be any evidence whatsoever. I was going to get in and out like a robbery even after stabbing him over thirty times. I could see it going down like a movie, introducing KeeKee; in, *"Death of a Teacher."*

Being that it was the alternative program, class started later in the day. I paced back and forth for a couple of hours ready to make my debut. I had the largest knife from the kitchen hidden under my shirt, watching the time as it ticked by. Up to this point, I had never killed anyone but that day he was going to be my first victim. By the time I made it to school he was already there, so I was going to catch him leaving. As I sat in my car with the knife in my lap, minutes turned to one hour and my anger went from five to seven. That's when the police pulled on the side of me. "Excuse me ma'am is everything alright."

I gripped my knife but kept it on my lap. I smiled, "Yes officer, I'm waiting on a friend. She's in the alternative program. She started last week and the times she gets out vary, so I'm here early, so I won't be late."

"Ok young lady. I was just checking because I saw you sitting here earlier. Well, be safe."

He then drove off. I had now panicked and started my car to leave. I gave the building one last peek through my rear view mirror and that's when I saw the teacher standing in the door way. He was getting ready to leave. I cut my car off so fast. I then thought about it and started my car back up so I could have an easy get away. I grabbed the knife and got ready to exit my car. I saw him walk up one stair then another stair. I was like a dog in heat because I was ready to hop on him and attach my knife to his body back to back. He got to the top stair then he turned around and went back into the building with another

The Fight Was Worth It

teacher. So I started praying, "If this is meant let him come back out." So as I set there waiting on him to come back, two, three, and five minutes turned into fifteen, twenty, and thirty minutes. The next thing I know he was passing me in his car. He normally parked his car where I was parked, but this day in particular he parked on the other side. I left without incident, and the weight was lifted off my shoulders.

The Fight Was Worth It

Dad and Daughter Talk

I realized that everything happens for a reason. What God brought me through was much bigger than getting kicked out of school. I needed to do something quick, because I was headed back into the pathway of destruction.

One day as the Lord was dealing with my heart, He sent my dad in to speak with me. My dad and I sat and talked for about two hours. My dad did the talking as I actually listened. I was hearing about Christ and I did not get angry. The person that I invented within myself was now being convicted and it felt good. Even though I felt convicted my pride kept me from letting my dad know that he was finally reaching me. Yeah, the event was humbling but that does not mean it burnt away all pride. I told my dad, "God probably does exist, but sometimes when certain things don't go the way I planned, that's when I feel like He doesn't."

The last thing my dad told me in that conversation was, "Well I have said all I could say. If you don't believe me God will send someone else to tell you the exact same things that I'm telling you. KeeKee I'm going to say this and I'll leave it alone. The day you almost died, who do you think saved your life? It wasn't the devil because he wanted you dead."

The Fight Was Worth It

I Gained Insight, During Real Talk

After that talk, I realized that my life was like putting together pieces of a puzzle. But, there were two major pieces missing. Those missing pieces kept my puzzle from becoming a masterpiece. The two missing pieces were, me totally letting go of my ways and letting God be the head of my life.

It was now time for me to head to work. Upon arrival I was asked to cover a table full of females for another waitress. As I waited tables there was this guy on one side and the females were sitting diagonal of him. The guy was telling me about Christ, while the females were speaking about witchcraft. I was telling the women, "Yeah that's how I believe." And I was telling the guy, "Yeah that's what my parents been telling me."

At this point I was torn between the truth and a lie. I was confused whether I should remain a sinner or start going to church. As I got ready to walk away, the guy said something that won me over. This complete stranger told me, "Somebody told you that God would send someone to tell you the same things they were telling you. I'm that person that God sent so come visit my church."

He gave me the address to his church. At that moment it was no longer a question of whether or not God existed. My body almost went limp. I ran into the restroom and cried like a baby. That Sunday my car was loaded with my brother and a few friends. When we walked in the

The Fight Was Worth It

church we felt like we were high on drugs because the anointing was so strong. That was the first day of my journey in the Lord and no one had to pump or prime me to go. How did I know that I was ready to give my life to Christ? It's like when a man finds a wife, he just knows.

The Fight Was Worth It

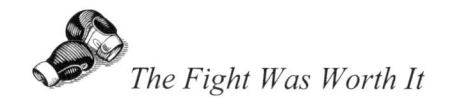

Definition of a Christian Please

I was going to church regularly. I had been baptized, and I felt liberated. I was on cloud nine and no one could get me down. Everything I was praying about was coming to pass. God was certainly proving His power now. Not too long ago, I was trying to convince others that there was not a God. But now, I was trying to convince people that God did exist. I was taking my newly found faith more seriously.

However, there were many days I was misled by the actions of fellow Christians. I saw stuff that had me questioning whether I should take this walk as seriously as I originally did. I quickly learned that people wanted a position in the church but didn't want the responsibility that goes along with the position.

The Word says "all fall short," and folks were running with that scripture. I witnessed people cursing, drinking, smoking, lying, talking about others, and shacking up. There were devious pastors and I've even witnessed something foul from a first lady, it seemed like the church was the new "hot spot."

I started to think that all Christians were hypocrites. The background that I had come from called for me to be around people that would encourage my walk, not people reassuring me that Christianity is pointless. No one was really telling me anything or guiding me in the right

The Fight Was Worth It

direction to fully live out my Christian walk, and that was sad. Instead of being partnered with strong spiritual counselors, I was getting partnered with some of the worst. How could the blind lead the blind? At the time I did not understand the scripture that tells us to 'study to show thyself approved,' so I based my life off what I saw, and spiritually, I was becoming unstable. My church counselors had nothing good to say, while it seemed as though the only thing the pastor had to say was, "Come to church and give your money so God could bless you." I was giving faithfully so I was getting blessed financially. Just imagine what could have happened if they spoke against sin.

I tried to hold on to my faith but it was hard. I was led to worship both God and a stone because I was almost convinced that God could not do it alone.

I started going to a new church but it was the same old thing. The more hypocrisy I saw, the less serious I was about Christ. I didn't know much about sin, but I did have a notion that we should not be doing the same things we did when we were of this world.

I started reading the Word for myself trying to learn more about sin. I did not understand what I was reading. I did not understand why Jesus spoke in parables. Then I got to thinking, 'Why Jesus could not just say what He was meaning?'

But I did understand when the Word says, 'He spoke that way so those that are His could understand.' Then I got to thinking, 'But I belong to Jesus too so why do I not understand it. One scripture says one thing, and

The Fight Was Worth It

another scripture says something else is one lying?' I was like, "Come on Bible!" I was on a verge of a spiritual death. Before I realized it, I had gotten so frustrated with the Bible that I ripped it in half and threw it across the room. I started crying and yelled "This Bible is a lie! That's why I did not believe!"

I went wrong when I tried to impress man over God. I went wrong when I stopped answering to God and started answering to man. Man will fail us but God will never fail us. However at the time, I didn't know that.

So after that incident I was listening to secular music again. I thought it was okay to listen to secular music because my pastor did not see anything wrong with it. Listening to secular R&B music had me thinking about sex on a regular, and I was ready. Once during new membership's class the pastor spoke on fornication, but I guess he forgot who he was talking to and he said, "Sex is good, I mean so so good."

Here the pastor was telling a group of single people that sex was good. Was he expecting us not to want to fornicate? Okay… If that was the plan, he failed. He said something about marriage, but after hearing how good sex is…I was thinking of a sex plan. I wanted to experience sex more now than ever. With all that was going on I was slowly drifting back into sin.

The Fight Was Worth It

Touch of Hurt

I started acting on a sexual desire that I had for some time. That desire was for other women. I was ready to be an open lesbian. I knew exactly who I wanted so that was not the problem. My problem was that I was not too sure if she would bust my head for coming on to her, or if it would be a touchdown. She was a longtime friend of mine but nothing she did ever hinted that she would like rubbing rocks together… until one day I caught her in a lesbian act.

I was on my way to bed and I heard what sounded like two females arguing outside of my window. When I looked out my window, I was aroused when I saw the girl that I wanted and another girl locking lips. The girl that I wanted said, "It is over" at the end of the kiss.

I was over thrown with excitement because I was about to make my move. Seeing this girl kissing another girl jolted a volt of lust for her that had me wanting to make out with her right then and there.

However, it also triggered a flash back that reminded me why I was attracted to females in the first place. I experienced something at a very young age that affected my life mentally and physically. Although I forgave the person, there were some days that a flash back would knock me off track like a rushing wind. I would have flash backs of how every weekend my brother and I would get an early start. We would always be awakened to the smell of

The Fight Was Worth It

bacon, or sausage, eggs, rice and or grits. After breakfast, we would bathe and get dressed. My Mom would always have my brother and I dressed so beautifully. My hair would always look as if I was fresh from the beauty salon finished with a bow. My shorts would always coordinate with my shirt and shoes. A compliment from the neighbors was normal for me and my brother.

My brother and I would play outside as our parents sat on the porch. There were very few children our age in the neighborhood, so we didn't have many friends. One day my brother and I watched as my mother's associate and her family moved into the apartment complex next door. She had two children as well. As time progressed, her daughter adopted me as a play daughter, while the son wanted to play house with me when my parents were not looking. He would tickle me so much that I was uncomfortable, but I could not help but laugh. I was a young girl attracted to that older boy. I had a habit of sitting with my legs opened. One day I noticed that his head was almost glued towards my "pleasure box." I was about to become a victim of a heinous crime.

Earlier that day the sun was shining and there was a cool summer's breeze beating against my body. As day turned to night, I set outside making mud pies while my brother slept and the adults played cards on the front porch. I was now exhausted and about two minutes away from empting my bladder right there. I was taught not to use everybody's toilet so I didn't know what to do. Although we lived next door, we lived on the top floor in the apartment complex, so I knew I was not going to make it there. I started squirming. My mom said, "Girl let me take her home," but our neighbor offered her restroom since it was closer and told me I could rest on the couch. My mother asked was anyone in the house. The neighbor said her daughter was but she was asleep, her son was down the street somewhere, and her boyfriend was at work. My neighbor was unaware that her son was in the house and about to change my life almost forever.

As I entered their home, the smell of mothballs greeted my nose. In the front room set the neighbor's son on a plastic covered couch. The loveseat and recliner were also covered with plastic as an accessory. There were out of place VCR tapes and a VCR on a glass table surrounded by wood. As I passed the kitchen, I noticed chairs were out of place, and dishes were scattered all over the table and sink. There were roaches commuting along the walls as if they had a place to go. I was starting to get sick to my stomach. The floor looked like it was in desperate need of a broom and mop. Before I could reach the restroom, all I could hear in my head was my Mom saying, "You can't use everybody's toilet" and now I was regretting the decision to use their restroom.

I finally made it into the restroom. The first thing I noticed was the aroma of urine as strong as ammonia. There was still water in the tub. There was a ring around the tub and it appeared as if all four of them had taken a bath in that same water. The mirror had smears as if they rubbed butter on it. I got to thinking, 'I have come this far so either I use their toilet, or let the urine leak down my legs.' So I got to thinking, Mom said if I just have to use somebody else's toilet, don't sit down, stand up.'

So, that's what I did. I made it to the toilet, and as I finished the door swung open with force. The same person that seemed so gentle at first had now become creepy while he was staring at me with my shorts down. Startled, I told him I was not finished yet and I pulled my blue shorts up. He shut the door, grabbed me, and pushed me against the door. I could smell and feel his hot breath as he tried licking me in my mouth. He was wrestling to get my clothes off. I was scratching him while he

The Fight Was Worth It

was trying to cover my mouth and pull my shorts down. I was screaming asking him to stop but he ignored my cries as he punched and pushed me. My Mom and neighbor thought I was asleep, but I was in the house fighting for my virginity. Once he got my shorts down he tried but was unable to insert his penis inside of my "pleasure box" so he used his finger.

A cry screeched out of my mouth as this pain shot through my body faster than sound travels, and I dropped to the floor. Once this monster noticed the blood he said, "If you tell anyone I'll kill you!"

And he walked away. His sister never heard a thing because she was asleep with the television blasting. I'm not sure what pleasure he got out of the whole ordeal but he left my "pleasure box" painfully uncomfortable, and he caused me to shed innocent blood. I remember sitting in the restroom crying, trying to wipe my "pleasure box" and panties clean of any blood stains. After that day I was not the same and neither was he. I remember he tried molesting me again and I said "No" and I told him I was going to tell. He planted his teeth into my skin and after shaking his head like a dog he detached a plug from my leg. He reminded me never again to say a word about what happened. Even when we moved, there were guys trying to molest me. After being hurt physically, mentally, and emotionally by males, I knew I did not want to be touched by another male again.

Years later I tried moving forward and leaving my past behind me. Homosexuality was not considered the norm like it is today, so I had to put on an Oscar winning heterosexual performance. I was attracted to females, but I would occasionally kiss and touch certain males. After a

The Fight Was Worth It

while I was actually attracted to males again, until I was double crossed.

One day I was on my way home from school and I noticed this guy that I knew well, following me with a blank look on his face. He had his hand in his pants a little too long which seemed weird if not suspicious. I spoke to him but he didn't speak back, and I was not about to speak again. This dude was super creepy that day.

Once we got near the train tracks he caught up with me and said he wanted to talk. We ended up sitting on someone's stairs. Immediately after sitting down he pulled out his "pleasure stick" and then asked me to touch it. When I refused his advances he got extremely upset. He then pushed me back and rushed on top of me. While he was wrestling to get my clothes off, I was screaming and fighting with the agonizing fear of losing my virginity at an age, and in a way that I never planned on losing it.

While I was screaming for him to get off me, he was screaming back, "I been waiting for this for a long time, and today you gone give me some!"

I could not believe that I was about to be raped in somebody's front yard in broad daylight. With one last option, I grabbed, twisted, pulled and he got off me. I bet he was not expecting for me to touch his "pleasure stick" in that way. Totally lost at what just happened I took off running. The dude then got up holding his self and yelled, "I'm gonna shoot and kill you the next time I see you."

The Fight Was Worth It

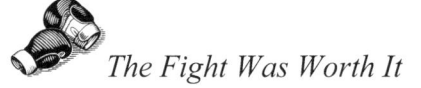

For years I feared for my life. Even though I was the victim, he made me feel like he was the victim. My dislike for guys had now been elevated to disgust. After that day I made up my mind that I would never trust another man again.

The Fight Was Worth It

Not Even Ten Years Old

Broken dreams and emptiness
Low self-esteem and fear
Crying out within myself
Hoping someone hears
As I whispered softly
Asking you to stop
But even in my courtesy
Your heart remained solid as a rock

You took a piece of me
That part I would never get back
All you wanted to do
Was satisfy yourself

I was just a little girl
How could you be so cruel?

Not even ten years old yet
When my innocence you abused
You touched me in hurtful ways
And asked me to keep quiet
But the pain you unleashed on me that day
Had me wishing I could die in it…

You caused me to be evicted from reality
Hopelessness was now my mentality
Because you told me you were doing me a favor
Because nobody else would want to touch me.

I believed your lies for a moment

The Fight Was Worth It

Until Christ got a hold of me
And showed me that I was victorious
And that was just wicked of you
To take a piece of me!

I'm no longer haunted by my past!
Today I stand and share my story
I call it this
'When predators attack'
And you are the malicious advocate in it

Then you tricked me into believing
That it was my fault…

You convinced me that my family would disown me
But then you contradicted yourself by saying if I told
You would kill me

So I,
I kept quiet

As you kept your pride.

I have been silent long enough
But on today I will separate truth
From lies

I am standing up for females
All across the world
No matter who your abuser is
Let your voices be heard
Sexual abuse is not your fault
But they would make you think so

I was not even ten years old yet
So what about sex did I know?

He touched me with his hands
Making me feel nasty

The Fight Was Worth It

Disgusted with myself as he said he was doing me a favor
But how I felt
He never did ask me…

As tear after tear fell from my eyes
My abuser attacked me and watched
Me cry

I was just an innocent little girl
The day my abuser changed my world

But from here on out my story I'll tell
What he did to me caused regret, anger, and fear
Didn't know who to trust
Because my heart was pierced

If you are a victim
As I was too

Forgive your abuser
Then give it over to Jesus
So he could heal you

Don't be ashamed
Because Jesus can fix it

And I stand here
Telling my story as a witness

My abuser took a piece of me
But he did not take my soul
Glory be to God
As your healing starts to flow
Glory be to God!

The Fight Was Worth It

Closer Than Friends, She Was My Lover

Now as an adult with raging hormones I was about to step on to the other side. Flashbacks of my past kept me in bondage. I made up my mind that I was going to live my life as a male, and no one was going to stop me. I felt like I was born in the wrong body and I hated it. Since I felt like I was in the wrong body, for me to become a male would not be a sin. I felt like God made a mistake when He made me. Everything about me screamed out male- from the way I acted, to the way I walked, and even my desires. Then, the way I wore my hair plus the way I dressed was like a replica of a boy, and even the way I looked. Mentally I was trying to blame God for me being a homosexual, but emotionally I was just tired of being hurt by males.

I was ready to pursue my relationship. I now knew the girl that I wanted was a homosexual so I made my move, and she denied me. I could not believe it. She said she see me only as a friend and plus she was not like that. When I told her I knew the truth she was bashful, but later that night she was my girlfriend. Our first kiss had me wondering if I was under her spell. We instantly connected. Whatever I asked of her, she gave it to me. Wherever I wanted to go, she went-even to church with me.

The Fight Was Worth It

She would dance for me, turning me on like a light. Whenever we were together I felt like I was living and I got so much joy from this girl. Not too long after we got together she started touching me in ways that I had never let a guy. When she touched me everything about it felt right. I would go to sleep and dream about this girl. I felt like this was of God maybe even an ordained relationship.

We would be in the store kissing and touching not caring what people thought. When we were in the car waiting on the red light to turn green we would lock lips sometimes until the car behind us honked. We felt like we were in love but it was mere lust. We started to get more comfortable with each other so we took our relationship to the next level. We were now taking part in an immoral act that had us contemplating marriage. There were times that we could not wait to leave church to sin. We would pull off the church lot and onto another lot just to commit what felt nothing like sin. She would call me sometime just to say, "I'm hungry."

Whenever my girlfriend would say that, I knew what she meant and I was heading out of the house like an illusionist. As she would touch me I could feel the chills climbing my body as if she was my spider and I was her web. After the sexual contact started we were inseparable. I found everything that I thought I needed in her. We started sitting out in the cold and snowy weather together for hours as I became "her flute." When it was time for her to go home I would drop her off and before I could get home she was calling. We would sometimes talk until the sun came up and repeat it all again the next day.

The Fight Was Worth It

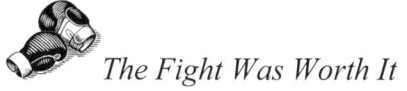

After a while my Dad and Mom started having their suspicions so they addressed the situation using wisdom and the word of God. My parents told me they would not disown me but they rather for me to do it the way God asked, since I was now a Christian. I vehemently denied the allegations but my behaviors displayed something totally different. That was one dirty little secret I was willing to hide as long as I could. I did not want to disappoint my supportive parents, but I did not want to lose the only other person that loved me. The church was not speaking against it. Our church mentor was more interested in our sex life than telling us the truth, and again it felt right. So how could it be wrong? I felt like God was in control so if this was wrong, why did He allow me to fall in love with a woman? Meanwhile, I failed to comprehend that God gives us a free will to choose good or evil.

The Fight Was Worth It

DIRTY LITTLE SECRET

Y ou hurt me
Crushed my heart
And almost tore me apart

You were thirsty after my blood to destroy me
And leave me lying there helplessly

Hungry to eat away at my soul
While you transform my thoughts
From His to mine
And from mines to yours

You gave me guilty pleasures
And had me coming back for more

Absent from now, long gone from then
As I try to erase my thoughts of you
The time I had with you becomes more fulfilling

I lust after you
You have dominated my feelings for you
And you have completed me at times as you filled me up

With the essences of you
I could have had my cake and ate it too

You're Sin
But how can I let you go
Because you are so jaw dropping at times

The Fight Was Worth It

Filling my mind
Every piece of my mind with thoughts of you

I am desperate to find another way
But you are so deceitful
That I have become fond of you

Sin oh sin
I see the beast that has
Has become of me because of you

Sin
Sin you were my dirty little secret
But now I have to let you go

The Fight Was Worth It

Can I Live Without Her

My parents were adamant when talking to me about my faith and relationship. My parents would often tell me that God does not approve of my lifestyle. I would tell my parents, "I am happier than I've ever been so I don't think it's wrong."

And they would say, "You are your happiest because you have accepted Christ now. You could be even happier if you do it just the way He is telling you."

"Well He's not telling me to leave her alone, y'all are."

"Yeah, but God would also use people to speak a word. God made Adam and Eve not Adam and Steve."

"Well the people at church are not saying anything about us"

"I tell you what, if you don't believe us, seek God, He'll let you know what to do."

"How?"

"Just pray about it. Pray that God reveal the truth to you concerning your relationship. You know how to pray."

Daily I prayed but I did not receive any immediate answers. I believe it took so long because I was praying for God to let my parents know that this girl was right for me.

The Fight Was Worth It

Once I humbled myself and was willing to receive the truth from God, that's when He showed up and showed out. He showed me in His Word basically that homosexuality is an abomination to Him (Leviticus 18:22 and Leviticus 20:13). I repented, and asked God to take those homosexual desires away. As I was waiting for God to take those desires away from me, my heart felt like there was a blow torch being held to it. I loved this girl too much to walk away, but the reality of the matter was that I loved God more, so I could not stay.

Two days later I called it quits. I told my parent's in front of the church all that I had done. My parents forgave me. Instead of the church embracing me and encouraging me, they talked badly about me and told people outside of the church what I had done. Although they talked about me, I was free! I ended up leaving that church for unrelated reasons.

The Fight Was Worth It

DEAR GOD

God, God, how can I talk to you
When I am feeling this way?

I have done an injustice to you
In so many ways.

I really don't know if I should say I'm sorry
Because I'm bound to sin again
And I don't want my apology
Tainted with lies because what if I died in my sins?

It's like it's harder now
That I'm saved
Than it was back then

I'm losing my attraction to you
As my life is becoming grim

And I'm so thankful that you are interceding
Interceding on my behalf
Because if it wasn't for you interceding for me
I know that I would be dead

Because too often it's my flesh
Not my spirit being fed
So I'm dying from hunger
In need of spiritual bread

The Fight Was Worth It

I know it's worth it
Worth it for me to change my ways
And I know I need your help
But where I am right now, Lord
I find it hard for me to pray

But why do I forsake you, Jesus,
When you have never
Forsaken me?

My battle is not with you
But my battle is with me
Because I know trials come but to make me strong
Yet I keep falling weak
As if I'm subject to the Devil's defeat

But My God, you sit high and look low
My heart is in the right place
I know this you know
But it's like my flesh over taking me
Over taking me to go back to sin

I guess my battle is so hard now
Because I just cover my sins
Instead of getting some deliverance

It's like I'm ready to break
And changes are not coming fast enough
So I'm losing my faith
I want to return to the way I used to love you

Then, I stayed on my face
And I didn't sin as much back then
Because my heart was emerged in your love
And I honored your grace

The Fight Was Worth It

But now I've come to a place
Where I sin more freely
Because I lost focus of your direction
When you were trying to lead me

I allowed pride to get in the way
It easily deceived me
And my soul not my flesh was dying daily

In all reality
I'm tired of living this way
Not reading my Word and it's a battle to pray

I know who you are
I know what you've done
And yes I believe you're the only begotten Son
And you died and were resurrected

You are the new covenant in which I am directed
And if I do it any other way it's the Spirit I'm vexing
So I desire to apply Your Word to my life
By reading the Word daily, praying
And asking that you give me the appetite
To hunger after you with no ifs, ands, or maybes

Where I thought I was unchangeable by nature
Your purpose changed me
It took an intervention from the Spirit of God
To expose the enemy
Still had some residue there
That was hindering me

But now I have wisdom through you
And it is more profitable than silver
And yields better return than gold

The Fight Was Worth It

And now that I know the truth
I can't keep quiet
I have to speak boldly
The devil will not destroy my soul
That I speak in Jesus name
Glory be to God
That I'm not the same
Glory be to God

The Fight Was Worth It

Introducing William

May 21, 2000, five months after breaking it off with a female, I was headed to one of Saint Louis's annual parades. This parade could have been called the parade of lust because females would wear just enough to cover what needed to be legally covered. I was about to fall into a trap because I felt the only way I was going to feel like a female was to wear something revealing. However, the Lord told me not to put on anything revealing. I ended up putting on some blue jean loose shorts, with a blue shirt, white buddy shoes with red shoe strings. Once I made it to the parade I remember thinking, 'here I am a homosexual trying to live the life of a heterosexual.' As I walked through the crowd with my head down too ashamed to hold it up, the melody of a voice echoed my ears asking for my phone number. Immediately the Lord said he would be my husband. I loved to write so I kept a pen and paper. Going on faith I instantly grabbed the pen and paper out of my pocket and we exchanged numbers.

At that point I started doing a body scan. First I scanned his shoes. He was wearing all black name brand tennis shoes that looked like he had them for about three days at the most. I was thinking, 'Okay nice.' He sported black jeans that fit him enough to rock that sexy sag. He wore a gray t-shirt with black writing. I scanned his teeth, then his nails and I was thinking, 'Okay, this dude certainly takes care of himself, and I like it. He's a clean dude.' I saw that he had a perfect afro that was naturally curly and it matched his clothes- gray and black. He was tall and skinny with a beer in his hand. I was thinking, 'Okay, okay…Shoes, clothes, and body scan was a plus. Now let me see what his face looks like.'

The Fight Was Worth It

He was dark like my ex-girlfriend so that was a plus, but to my surprise he was ugly. I was thinking, 'Wow all that and this face, okay.' I started to walk away because I was just too out done, but as I walked away he grabbed my hand. When he grabbed my hand, it was like I had truly been touched by an angel because he had the softest hands known to mankind. He asked me if I was going to call him and I told him that I wouldn't he asked for my number.

We went our separate ways. Sometime later as I was leaving the parade I noticed a car rolling along side of me. When I looked it was him on the passenger side so I smiled and he said, "You didn't tell me your name, and it's not on this paper."

"I know William, just in case you lost it I didn't want people playing on my phone."

"I'm not going to lose it. So what's your name?"

"Smiley, or you can call me KeeKee."

"I like Smiley."

"Well William, I will call you Billy." Then I noticed he had a car full of kids in the back seat. So I got to thinking, 'And this is the dude that God said I will marry? My parents will never accept him and I'm not too fond of him either.' I smiled again. All I could hear was T.L.C singing, "I don't want no scrub."

The Fight Was Worth It

Call It What You Want

It was something about his smile that tickled my heart though. With all the bad, the good was that God said he would be my husband. So that night I was excited in anticipation for his call. William called me around 8:30 that night. As we talked I was thankful to learn the children in the back seat were not his. He told me he didn't have any children and none on the way. He told me a year earlier he tried to holler at me, but I told him I was interested in someone else. He said that I was beautiful several times that night.

He lived two blocks up from me and saw me all the time. But oddly enough, that was my first time seeing him. We had much in common and yet we were so different. I realized that we were just an oxymoron to each other. We were opposites, but together we were going to work just right. As we talked, it seemed like I had known him for years. Without hesitation, I told him that God said he will be my husband and he responded, "That can't be true Cuzz, I don't plan on getting married. I'm gone get high and hustle for the rest of my life and I don't need a wife for that."

I was thinking, 'And this is who God said I will marry? Man he is cold as ice. But God said it.'

Yeah he was cold but I loved him already because he was real with me. During another conversation I told

The Fight Was Worth It

him I wanted his baby and he blurted out, "Yeah, what they say about you is true, you is crazy."

Then sometime later I told him that I loved him but he didn't say it back. When I asked him if he love me, he gave me a response that had me melting in embarrassment. I never saw it coming. He said, "No I don't love you, but I like you. I ain't gone lie to you. But if you wanted me to fall in love with you, get your tongue pierced."

I was instantly turned on by his honesty. Although my dad previously told me not to get my tongue pierced, that was not going to stop me this time. Up to this point other than the day I got high I have always done what my parents asked of me. I loved William and I wanted him to love me. So the next day I got my tongue pierced. When my dad found out he was hurt because he seemed to think somebody would get the wrong impression of me. I was trying to build my relationship with William, not destroy it, so I cared less what others thought of me. It was like William kept his word because after the piercing we started spending more time together, and he started confiding in me more. He told me where he was, what he was doing, and who he was about to do. He told me many times that he wanted to have sex with other girls but he liked me too much to do so. I enjoyed every minute of this until he went cut throat. This dude asked me to try out my tongue ring on him. I was like, "What! I ain't down with that! You got me messed up!"

But I did not particularly use the word "messed." My dad was right this dude thought I gave "oral pleasures." Then I got to thinking, 'He's going to be mighty upset

The Fight Was Worth It

when he finds out that I ain't into giving "oral pleasures" or having sex.' So, hoping to impress him I made a solo sex tape. While I trusted him enough to be the first person I willingly showed my "pleasure box" he was betraying me. I found out that the tape I gave him for his pleasure was viewed by other people. I was devastated, hot under the collar, ready to call it quits, but he convinced me that it was my fault. He told me he only did it to prove a point. William said he was trying to show me that I could not just make sex tapes for dudes that I did not know because there is no telling what they would do. He said I should have more respect for myself, I agreed and so we moved on.

The Fight Was Worth It

The Same with No Sex

Now that I had put it out there, he wanted sex. I was not ready. He asked me often and I kept beating around the bush. So one day he said, "Either you gone let me hit it or not. It ain't that hard of a decision."

Although we were in our twenties, I did not want to have sex until I got married. But I didn't want to lose him either. So while we were in the back yard he was smoking a blunt and I was watching the back of his head like a movie. I told William, "So William, I want to have sex with you, I do, but I also want to wait until I get married. So are you willing to marry me?"

He took a puff from his blunt and kept his back turned to me and said, "For sex? Nope. I told you I ain't getting married."

I was thinking man I messed up, so nervously I asked, "Are you upset?"

"Nope."

"Do I have to leave now?"

"Nope."

Let me remind you, his back is still turned. So I asked, "Do you still want to be friends?"

"Yep."

The Fight Was Worth It

"So did you know I was a virgin?"

"Nope."

"Do you have a problem with that?"

"Nope."

"Good, because I am going to wait until I get married. What do you think about that?"

"Nothing."

"So why are you giving me all these one word answers? What do you really think about what I just said? Because, I know sex can make or break a relationship."

At that moment he took another puff from his blunt, blew the smoke out, and thumped it. As I watched the ashes from his blunt hit the ground he turned to me and said with a straight face, "You are blowing my high. Besides, we ain't no couple, and if we was, I'm willing to wait as long as you are."

He then lit a cigarette, took a puff, and blew the smoke in my face and said he was hungry. I stayed because he treated me to pizza. When I got ready to leave that night, he asked for a kiss and I told him I don't do that either. Later that night he called me and we talked like nothing happened. We were seeing each other every day from about eight in the morning until a little past midnight. We would go to the movies some weekends. He bought me clothes, shoes and food but not once did he ask for a hug, kiss, or

The Fight Was Worth It

sex in return. He did not even mention anything about the tape that I made, and I respected that.

The Fight Was Worth It

The Soul Ties

Seeing that he was different, I decided to offer him my "pleasure box" with no strings attached. I expected to be no more than two individuals with benefits. I was thinking, 'Sex can't change our lives that much,' but oh boy was I wrong.

I was nervous and excited at the same time. I was about to lose my virginity to a man that said he does not love me nor wanted to marry me. I could feel the butterflies in my belly trying to escape, as I laid there thinking, 'I sure hope he knows what he is doing because I sure don't.' As we were about to make it official my dad called for me to come home and cook. I slammed the phone down and yelled, "What! My dad has never asked me to cook before. Out of all days why today?"

The very next day William and I were at it again. As he started to penetrate me, I felt our souls connect. (The connecting of the souls is called soul ties) Once we finished he laid there and wrapped his arms around me and started talking. While he was talking I was thinking, 'Since he wants to cuddle, how long do we lay here before we shower? I would never forget this day. I'm a woman now. I love him so much more now. I wonder if he loves me now. Will he make me his girlfriend now? Does he want to marry me now? What is he thinking? Was it everything he thought it would be? I am now going to have sex with him for everyday that I wanted to have sex and I didn't. Was I

The Fight Was Worth It

his best or worst? Will he call me again? Did he like it? What does he think of me now? Will he tell anybody? Was he recording it? Did he use a condom? Does he have a sexually transmitted disease? Am I pregnant? That was so painful! I wonder is he going to want to have sex with me again since it was such a hassle getting his "pleasure stick" inside my "pleasure box." I am so sore. How am I going to be able to walk now? I wonder if he is the same way with other females that he has sex with. Will my parents know?'

A lot was going through my mind.

The Fight Was Worth It

Sex, So Be Gone

So after lying down for a while, he sat straight up on the bed and said something that shook the whole course of what just happened. "You remember when you said you wanted to wait until you got married to have sex,"

I said, "Yeah, why you say that?"

I then set up and started putting on my clothes so I could go home and shower. Then he said, "That's what they all say"

My whole body went numb, and just for a moment I had an out-of- body experience. I finished getting dressed and as we walked from the basement to the front door, I felt like a dog with its tail tucked between its legs. It was like William threw a curve ball flying one hundred thirty miles per hour at my glass world. What I thought we had was now shattered. I never saw it coming. With all the embarrassing comments he has made to me up to this point, this has to be by far the most embarrassing. Once we got to the front door I asked, "So what does that mean? Will you ever call me again?"

And he assured me that he would. After I got home, many thoughts went through my head. Not only did he bring pain to my "pleasure box," but he broke my heart. My emotions had parachuted right past my feelings being hurt. I was devastated! I could not believe I was deceived! I

The Fight Was Worth It

could not understand why God would lie to me like that. I was furious. My emotions led me to believe he deserved to die for this! I gave him my body, all that I owned, and he treated me this way!

The Phone Call

As I lay there on the couch weeping in my sorrow and ready to drink my life away the phone rang. I did not recognize the number, but hoping it was William I answered it. It was William on the other end. The first question he asked was, "Did you think I was going to call?"

"No."

"But I did call."

"I see."

As we talked on the phone that night he called me a broad, chick, and a chicken head. He called me all kinds of names. Every time he called me a name I would correct him and then he'd call me a different one. The sweetest name that he called me that night was "his girl." We started the night out as sex partners and ended the night as a couple.

The Fight Was Worth It

Our World Verses the World

The day we had sex was the day our life took a drastic shift. I was overtaken by this spirit that had caused me to be a crazed, jealous, maniacal, violent girlfriend. Once we fornicated, that opened the door for sin. My jealousy had me threatening him not to look at other females. My jealousy was out of control. Whenever I saw a female that I thought he may find attractive, I would check to make sure his "pleasure stick" was still asleep. Whenever we watched television and somebody would kiss or have sex I would check to make sure his "pleasure stick" was still asleep.

My craziness had me accusing him of cheating even though we were spending every day and all day together. I became extremely devious by doing whatever I thought it took to keep him home and assure that he would never leave me. I would cut his clothes up and poke holes in his condoms, but every time he would catch me. I started being controlling even to the point where I did not want him to shower unless I was there. He had to talk on the phone with me until he fell asleep and call me as soon as he got up. William loved playing video games and when I felt like it was getting more attention than me, I would destroy the system. He had a 'Dreamcast' and I destroyed it. He had a 'Play-station' and 'X-Box 360' and I destroyed them both. I did not want to share William with anything or anybody including his mother and sister. I worshipped William. In my mind there was '**our world**', the world that we shared

The Fight Was Worth It

with each other and no one was able to come into it. Then there was '**the world**' that was the part of our life that only I could share with others like co-workers, shoppers, classmates, ect. If at any time William would step outside of '**our world**' and into **'the world'**, I would try to cause him the most hurt that I could think of. I was losing it. I felt like a psycho but I couldn't help it.

The Fight Was Worth It

Beat Me Up Please

It had been a while since I cut or burned myself, but the desire for painful pleasure had resurfaced. I would ask for strange request during sex because the pain made it more pleasurable. He started noticing my problem and when I asked him to try his hand at burning himself he thought I was crazy. But in my mind, I was pretty normal and he had the issue because he didn't want to do it. I was feeling worthless. I was questioning whether or not William loved me. He didn't seem to care if I was there with him or not. I felt like the only way for me to feel like I meant something to William was for him to show signs of jealousy, or beat me. He refused.

For weeks I was trying to get him to beat me but he just wouldn't. I would grab his hand forcing him to punch me in my face. Then I started punching him for no reason at all, hoping to soon reap what I was sowing. After getting tired of being punched he finally hit me. The day William hit me my heart sung out like an opera. It was beautiful. Although once he bashed me it was like making love because it felt good, there was just more to it. In my mind, he was so sweet because he was now beating on me. For him to beat me was symbolic to him telling me he loved me and did not want to live without me. With every punch I would hear, 'If I can't have you, no one can.' For me, getting beat meant he had control over me and I was ready

The Fight Was Worth It

to be controlled. I did whatever I could so he'd keep beating me. Our lives were turned upside down.

The Fight Was Worth It

Sex in the Morning, in the Evening, and at Supper Time

Every day-but not particularly in this order,-we would fornicate, he would get high, maybe sell some drugs, and we'd top it off with a fight. He was going to church because my parents asked him to, but his heart was far from the church, I knew because he told me so. I was no better because I was drinking hypocrite juice. To my parents I was an innocent little girl, but William knew the beast that was inside of me. Sometimes during service when I noticed that he was focused on the Word, I would whisper in his ear, "After service I want you to beat it up." I knew from that point on, all he could think about was sex. My mission was accomplished.

I was a sex fanatic. I woke up thinking about sex. I went to sleep thinking about sex. Whenever I ate in front of William I made it sexual. That "pleasure stick" of his was a wand that tricked me into believing I could not live without sex. The only day we did not fornicate was the Sunday that he got baptized, but the next day we were at it again.

When I was not trying to sex him down we were fighting. To us, make up sex was the best sex so sometimes we would fight just to make up. We fought and had sex everywhere. Whether we were inside or outside we fought and had sex. Whether we were inside a car or on top of a car we fought and made out. Whether we were in the house or at a hotel we fought and had sex. Whether we were alone or had company, we would fight and make out.

      The more we had sex the more jealous and confused I got. The jealous part of me would have a problem with him talking to another female, even if she spoke to him first. If we were watching television and a woman came onto the screen I automatically thought he was going to cheat on me with her. So without any warning or solid reason I would unload a round of punches to his face. The confused part of me had me giving him the permission to visualize another woman while making love to me. Other times he would have to tell me what he liked about the other woman's body as we watched porn together. However, if I was not there, it was a demand that he did not watch porn. I had now reached insanity.

The Fight Was Worth It

Crazy KeeKee

I would use my prophetic gift to figure out the codes to his answering machine and speak to others he was around to find out if he was cheating. When we were not together, I would stalk him from the corner. If I had a dream that he was cheating I would get out of bed and stalk him through his basement window. I had the intent to do a lot of harm if I saw another female with him. With my dreams and his actions I assumed he was cheating, so I called my ex-girlfriend and became "her flute." As if that wasn't enough, one day after he threated to leave me, I knocked on someone's door and said that William had a gun, and was trying to break into their home.

The Fight Was Worth It

The Other Girl's Baby

Shortly after that incident I found out I was pregnant with our first child, Kashe'la. This was a shocker to both of us because doctors said I would not ever get pregnant. William instantly changed, he started working and I was telling everybody that William sealed the deal. While I was telling people about the pregnancy I overheard him telling his people not to say anything. I was puzzled because this was his first child, yet he didn't want anyone to know. So one day I was riding in the car with his family member and a friend of his. The friend said a name that sounded a lot like my unborn child's name. So I said, "I told Billy not to tell anybody our daughter's name."

The dude said,

"What you pregnant? That makes what, baby number two for Billy?"

"Naw this is our first child."

"Naw, I'm talking about my niece."

So Billy's family member jumps in the conversation to do a "cover up" but I was not trying to hear a word she was saying. I was thinking, 'You scan and William scan. Y'all knew he had a baby and I'm just now finding out about this while I'm pregnant. I asked him if he had any children and he said no. When I see him I'm punching him

The Fight Was Worth It

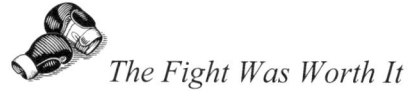

right in the face.' The ride home was very quiet. When I saw William I gave it to him, several blows to his face.

Since I found out that William lied to me about this other baby, I was about to hurt William in the worst way. I went to my longtime male friend's house and let him kiss the belly that carried William's baby. Then I let him rub my belly and talk to my unborn child. Finally, I hopped in the shower to receive "oral pleasures" from this man. In the middle of it, William called my cell phone and I told him I was over another dude's house in the middle of something. The guy told me to hang up the phone and when William called back, I did not answer. Once we finished he asked if he could "orally satisfy me" again the next day and I told him, "I'll see."

Then he asked if he could be there when I had William's baby and I told him, "Yes." When I went over to William's house the next day he was heated. He asked me if I had sex with the guy.

The only thing that kept William from cracking my head was our fetus that was growing on the inside of me. William said he did not want to see me that day so I left and I started thinking. 'What did I do? Here I am pregnant with William's baby but I let another man give me "oral pleasures." William has watched me go from 150 pounds to 180 pounds and instead of leaving me he finally told me he loved me. William has watched my flat stomach turn into a keg but I told this other man that he can watch me deliver. Man I got to get it together.' William and I never stayed angry at each other too long so things were back to normal the following day. As far as my pregnancy, the time flew

The Fight Was Worth It

by like a bird. Before we knew it, I was on the delivery table and William was right there holding my hand. I was having so many complications but William kept encouraging me to keep pushing. He'd say, "I love you! You can do it! Push! Our daughter is almost here! Baby don't give up! Here she comes! Here she come!" After she came out he shouted, "Thank you Jesus!" I remember him smiling and he said, "You did it! I could not have picked a better woman to be the mother of my children."

"No William, we did it."

I was on my last leg. I lost so much blood that I needed a blood transfusion. I had pushed so hard that around my eyes had swollen to the size of Tangerines. Our most terrifying moment by far, came when my body refused to deliver the placenta. Everything that could have gone wrong seemed to, but God brought us through it. That was the scariest and happiest day of our life. After I healed it was back to the same old stuff. My jealousy was multiplied by ten. I was thinking since I had his baby, he now owed me his undivided attention. I was worried about our relationship growing, not him bonding with our baby.

The Fight Was Worth It

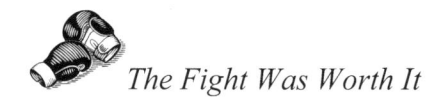

Attacking the Flesh

At this point I was almost completely out of control. I cursed like a sailor. I was drinking more than I ever did. I was smoking black and mild's like people drink water. I was getting angry more and more. I would black out and act on emotions, with no common sense.

When I got angry at William my mind would be set on getting back at him in the worst way possible. Many times I almost added murderer to my list of crazy behaviors. For example, there was one fight we had outside where I blacked out. The next thing I knew we were on the ground and I was hearing a voice say stomp his head into the ground. There was another time where he wanted to break off our relationship, but I told him, "If I could not have you no one would."

I remember chasing him down the street in my car with my mind set to critically injure him. All this foolishness started after we had sex. God says no sex before marriage for a reason. Fornication releases all kinds of unclean spirits. Our sin was now manifesting into a spirit of death.

The Fight Was Worth It

My Knife, His Gun

One day I was going over to see him and a girl was coming out the house. I blacked out. I was going to cut now, and ask questions later. All I could see was his "pleasure stick" in my hand, and me holding it up like a trophy. I was going to make sure that if he did cheat he would never do it again, and if he did not cheat he would never cheat. I ran in the kitchen grabbed a knife and went right for the "pleasure stick." He unloaded a blow to my face that snapped my head back like whiplash. I lost my balance and as I fell he knocked the knife out of my hand. I instantly started doing a horror movie scream as I ran straight towards the door and out the house. As I was running down the stairs I could feel my head swelling and the pain from the knot was throbbing like a heartbeat. I went straight to the police station and unfolded lie after lie on the table. When they asked what made him do it? I told them in my horror movie voice the best lie that I could think of, "He's crazy officer, he's crazy!"

Come to find out the female was the daycare driver. She was only in the house to get the children loaded onto the daycare van. After that day, William and I went about four days without a fight. Once everything was semi back to normal we were fighting again. I did everything I could to push William to his next level of crazy and one day I finally got it. He pulled out a gun on me. All I could do was look him up and down and laugh. Then I asked him, "How can you kill me when I'm already dead?"

The Fight Was Worth It

I hardly ever took William seriously because I knew he loved me too much to hurt me. My definition and his definition of love were much different. Mine involved hurt while his involved patience.

I eventually took William seriously when he showed me '*His Hands Were Created for Choking.*' There was one time he choked me until I passed out but I came back immediately afterwards. There was another time he choked me to the point where I learned to take him serious.

The Fight Was Worth It

LOVE MISSED

You grab me by my throat and you choked me
I'm gasping for breath as you hold me
And stop me from inhaling

I feel like I love you too much to walk away
But you have abused me once again
As you have everyday

I feel worthless
So really I won't be able to make it without you

You have made me who I am
So really how could I doubt you

You have committed adultery with my mind
Because even though you don't tell me
I know you would find
A woman that will
Please you in ways I never could
Then you laugh in my face
And tell me not to cry because you keep it real

But because you lie
That makes you as fake
As a three dollar bill

The Fight Was Worth It

I love you beyond measure
You hurt me beyond pleasure
You are colder than winter weather
So how could I miss your love
Whenever I would tell you I love you
You would say whatever
The day you walked away
You didn't hurt me anymore,
But you made me that much clever

The Fight Was Worth It

Sex in Exchange for Salvation

We were together now for almost two years. One day while having sex I was praying for God to change his heart. I was praying for God to change him because God had been convicting me. I was ready to change, but I was too afraid that he would walk away if I changed. Then I heard a voice say, "Do not have sex with him. He won't leave you or cheat on you."

Immediately I started battling with that inner voice. I started thinking, 'Oh yes he will. This dude is a thug. If I don't have sex with him he will find somebody that will. If I keep having sex with him maybe I could get him to give his life to Christ. If I keep having sex with him he'll want to change. I just had his baby there is too much to lose.'

I went on and on trying to convince myself that it was okay. So, I continued to lie there and allowed him to do to me what God told me not to. He knew something was wrong because he kept asking me if I was okay and I kept telling him "Yes." Once we finished all I could do was ask myself, 'What just happened?' The next day I was feeling better so I was ready to redeem myself. I suggested sex, and he said, "No."

I was ready to hit him because I thought he had cheated. Since the day we started having sex we have almost never missed a beat, so I could not understand why he would say no. So I echoed him, "No! No!" I walked in his face and repeated, "No! What do you mean no?"

The Fight Was Worth It

He explained something to me that I will never forget. He said he was ready to get his life in order because it didn't seem right anymore. That's when I remembered what God told me the day before. I shared with him what God told me, and he told me, "You should have listened." That day we did not have sex because we both felt convicted. A few days past and things seemed to be back to normal. We decided we would try again, but I received a phone call. The following day someone called him. Then with the final attempt, somebody called talking about God. Then we figured it out. Even though we were committed to each other, God does not honor sex of any kind, if it's not between a husband and wife. So therefore, God kept intervening.

By March 19, 2002, William and I had our share of trials. In the midst of sin God still covered our lives with His mercy and grace. (Thank you Jesus!) On March 19, as William and I sat outside he fired up a blunt while talking about changing his life. I was looking at him and laughing. I asked him where was this new look at life coming from? He did not know and neither did I.

The Fight Was Worth It

A Birthday to Celebrate God

After spending a little time in the back yard talking about God, he put his blunt in his pocket and we headed to Ponderosa to celebrate my mother's birthday. As we sat there eating, across from us was a group of Christians being bold for God. As this man walked past them one of the ladies said something to him about God and it brought unity with them and him. During that evening William wasn't saying much because he was in a zone listening to them. I was talking but he wasn't hearing me. Then the lady from the other table with the bold Christians started talking to us. She was staring at us nodding her head, and saying, "Yes, Lord. The time is now. The time is now."

She then started telling us what we were talking about in the backyard as if she had been there. So I asked her, "Are you a psychic?" I wanted to know because I have been dealing with psychics for a long time, but none have been on point like this.

So she tells me, "Oh no honey I'm a prophet."

"I have never heard of prophet. So what is the difference in a psychic and what you just did, because psychics tell you your future too?"

"Honey psychics are of the devil. They do it to get paid. Prophets are sent by God and can only tell you what God shows them."

The Fight Was Worth It

So, after a while the Lord showed her more "on point stuff" about me. Once she said William was going to be my husband she won me over. I called my brother, our friends, and everybody I could think of to meet the lady who did not know me, but knew so much about me. She then told us that she and her husband had their own ministry and service was on Wednesday and Saturday. I started thinking, 'Saturday, man that's the day I get funky drunk so I probably won't be able to make that one.'

Then she handed us her card and told us that if we could make it, we should come because the Lord had something for us.

Once they left we stayed and had a blast. Once we made it home I asked William if he was going to the program on Saturday and he told me that he would because there was something different about them. Then, William went into his pocket and pulled out his blunt. I said, "I knew it. You don't want to change."

"I do and I am. I'm about to get rid of this blunt."

"Wow! Are you serious?"

It was a complete shocker to me, because I've known him for almost two years and everyday William has gotten high. He has even put sex on hold to get high, but now he was throwing his blunt away. I could not believe it. That's when he said, "Yeah. I'm gonna do this. I have never felt like this before and I know the time is now."

So, from March 19 up to that Saturday, it was so hard from me. My flesh wanted what was sinful while he was killing his flesh for spiritual things. I wanted to get closer to him and he wanted to get closer to God. He was trying to move forward while I was trying to hold him back.

On April 09, 2002 he told me he was going to have to walk away from our relationship because I was a weight on his shoulders. On April 10, 2002 we went to service together. Once we got there the Spirit of the Lord was moving. People were receiving and being slain in the Spirit. The leader was telling people stuff that only God could have revealed.

Finally our leader called William up to the front. Our leader started praying for William. William hit the floor. He was hollering, curling up while holding his stomach, wobbling on the floor, and foaming from the mouth. It seemed like he swallowed some acid. This was a side of him that I had never seen. Up to this point he has always been so tough, but for the first time he was as weak as a new born baby. I was thinking, 'Who is this dude?'

I supported my man though. Once he stood up he turned to me and told me it was officially over unless I changed. When he told me it was over I felt lost. It seemed like I was blindfolded in a desert trying to find my way home. I wanted God to move on me. Our pastor then called me up for prayer. I was feeling broken, so the Lord was able to move.

The Fight Was Worth It

NEW SHOES

On April 10, 2002, I rededicated my life to Christ and William was delivered. The Lord spoke again to William that I was supposed to be his wife so he proposed to me that night at church and I said yes. My relative was visibly upset about the proposal and went on and on about it. My relative did not want any involvement with our marriage, or anything thereafter.

I told my relative that God told me on May 21, 2000 that I would be William's wife, so I was making the right decision. That Friday William and I were at the court house paying for our marriage license. As time went by God was cleansing William. William confessed his secrets to me. He stopped lying, drinking, smoking weed and cigarettes. He stopped selling drugs and ended up flushing his drugs down the toilet. He stopped cursing, watching horror movies and porn, and listening to secular music. We still weren't having sex nor was he beating on me.

He told all his homies that he was walking away from the street life. They laughed at him and told him he'll be back. While things were on the incline for William and me, our families were on the decline with accepting our soon to be marriage. Although our families were not accepting what God told us, we were going to do what God said whether our family liked it or not. Who knew better than God if we were supposed to be together? Man was

The Fight Was Worth It

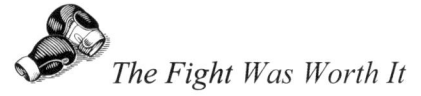

looking at our past while God was looking at what He was about to do in our lives.

The next in line to speak against our pending marriage was one of his relatives asking, "What would you do if the other girl's baby is proven to be yours? Your soon to be wife already said she wouldn't accept the baby so why would you marry her?" The individual then went on and on and ended with, "I just want you to be happy, and I think the whole marriage between y'all is a bad idea." Whatever negative words that could be spoken about our soon to be marriage, were spoken. There were people saying we should wait until we find a place to stay before we got married, because if we didn't it wouldn't work out. We would then ask them "Why wait when God said do it now?"

There were others telling us that we didn't have anything and wondered how our marriage would survive. But William said God promised to supply all our needs according to His riches and glory. William told people that he was determined to trust God. There was even a person that said one of us would end up dead, by the hands of the other. Within nine days instead of blessings being spoken over our union, people were speaking curses.

I was starting to have second thoughts as well. I did not want to marry someone that had a baby with another woman. But William assured me the baby wasn't his. William kept saying he was going to stand firm on what God told us. William was proven to not be the father of the other girl's baby.

The Fight Was Worth It

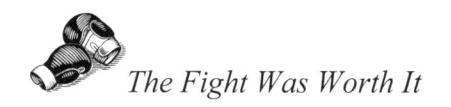

The Wedding

On April 19, 2002 I went from Ms. Collins to Mrs. Armstead at the court house. My mom, my dad, my brother, his friend, and my aunt were there. My husband's mom, her friend, and his sister were all there, and both sides were so happy for us.

As time went on I realized that the married life is hard! But William was willing to fight for our marriage with prayer and fasting.

The Lord told us He would use us in areas of our lives that we had not yet realized. He said we would have a music ministry but I was thinking, 'We can't rap, sing, or play instruments.'

He said we would travel the world, but I was thinking, 'I don't like to travel.'

He said William would speak to crowds of people and become a pastor. I thought 'If it's not me, William ain't gone talk to nobody.'

Then He said we would have a number of children together and I was thinking, 'It must be with another woman because I ain't gone have no more children.'

In three months God started blessing us because of our obedience. William was blessed with another job. We were blessed with a car and a home that was fully

The Fight Was Worth It

furnished. The blessings were overflowing. After much praying for me to be submissive to my husband's request to have another baby, we were blessed with our second child. God gave us the name Adiante'.

The Fight Was Worth It

Unhappy Happiness

In the beginning I rejoiced because I witnessed my husband being spiritually raised from the dead. The blessings felt good, the prophecy sounded great, but after a while his new lifestyle started to take a toll on me. I hated for him to put anything before me. At first he was putting video games before me so I got rid of all the systems. Then he started putting work before me so I made sure he lost his job. Now it was bigger than any of that. It was his Christianity that he was putting before me, and I felt the need to compete. My husband was a totally different guy than I met at the parade, and that bothered me. It bothered me so much so that I was going to make it my daily task to assure that he returned to sin.

I was always trying to find ways to accuse him or tell him that he had not changed. Plus, I still dealt with jealousy. I would check the history on the computer to see what sites he had viewed to have something against him, but I found nothing. I would set the television in a certain position so I could sneak in the front room and see what he was watching. If he would turn the channel before I saw what was on, I would punch him in his face. I was viciously attacking him, but yet, I was having a marital affair with the guy across the street. We were not having sex, but he was watching me and I was trying to keep his attention, because he already had mine. We knew the sexual tension was there because we talked about it. My eyes and thoughts were wandering. I would visualize what he was like in bed and I was hoping he was doing the same.

My biggest issue was not that I didn't love my husband, or it wasn't that I didn't know that he was a great man. My problem was I didn't know how to treat him. My insecurities had me walking down the road to a desperate house wife's avenue, because I wanted the best of both worlds.

I would feel beautiful as I watched different men lick their lips watching my hips sway as I walked. Meanwhile, in my mind, my husband had become distant, which meant he was cheating. I was working and he was working so I could not watch him all day. I started to speak a curse over his body for additional weight to be added. I didn't want anybody to be attracted to my husband but me. My husband's body structure went from 180 to an astonishing 450 plus pounds in like a year or two. I had no remorse what so ever. I felt it was justified because in this way I didn't have to compete with other females. The reality of the matter was this, what I thought was a problem had nothing to do with a female. My husband didn't want another female. My husband was becoming distant with me because he was drawing nearer to God spiritually.

While I wanted to talk about us, he wanted to talk about God all day, read his bible, and pray, which kept me feeling rejected. Not only was I feeling rejected but I was feeling disrespected when he would openly rebuke something and ask God for forgiveness. Every time he would rebuke something or ask for forgiveness, I would lay hands of violence on his head and face, then have the nerve

The Fight Was Worth It

to "get in his face," start pointing, and tell him the same line every time, "You ain't about to lust off no girl while I'm next to you and get away with it! I guarantee you, you ain't gone disrespect me!"

But he kept rebuking unclean thoughts and asking for God's forgiveness. For everything that I said to contradict what he was doing, he would refer to the Bible or ask me what Jesus would do? I didn't know and I didn't care what Jesus would do. But what I did know was it seemed like I had forgotten all about from where God brought us.

As a matter of fact, at that point, I was about tired of hearing about Christ. If it wasn't him, it was the people at church talking about Jesus. Everybody there knew I used to have a problem with hearing about the name of the Lord Jesus.

So, it seemed like this one lady would deliberately stand behind me just to test me. She would stand up during testimony service and thank Jesus for what I thought was the most unthinkable or petty things. Like no lie, she once stood up and counted it as a blessing because she found a dime. So I got to thinking, 'A dime lady? Really? Okay, you found that. I don't think He had anything to do with you finding a dime.'

I wanted to punch her in her face then rip my ears off for hearing what I thought was junk. While she was giving her testimonies boldly, I was keeping mine a secret. Not only that, but I stopped praying. I stopped worshipping God. Heck, I stopped acknowledging God altogether because I was too afraid to. It was like the enemy had confiscated my mind and replaced it with thoughts like his. I was led by the enemy to believe that if I lifted up the name of Jesus in any way, instead of men being drawn to Jesus, misfortune of every kind would be drawn to me. So, I was being mentally tormented once again to mock God. As for another example, the time I watched Passion of Christ, I tried to make myself cry to keep from laughing. I felt no passion for the Passion of Christ.

Speaking of passion, after a while my husband stopped having sex with me as often as I desired it. So one day I asked my husband for sex and he told me, "No."

I then told my husband with an attitude. "If you will not have sex with me, I just have to find someone that will. You remember that dude that gave me oral pleasures? He asked me today to let him do it. He said I won't owe him anything and guess what, that's where I'm headed now."

And I left the house on my way to commit adultery and bring a curse upon my family. I had never had sex with anyone but my husband, but that day I was willing to make an exception. I had it all planned out, after he gave me "oral pleasures" I was going to surprise him and share with him my "pleasure box." My husband did not chase me down the block or say a word. In the middle of the block I heard a voice ask me, "Is it worth losing everything?"

I immediately turned around. Once I got home I asked my husband why didn't he chase me and he said with

The Fight Was Worth It

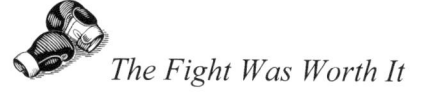

tears in his eyes, "I prayed about it and I was trusting God that you would not cheat."

With tears in my eyes I hugged my husband and said, "I'm sorry William and I thank you. I truly thank you for praying for me."

"You're welcome. You're my wife. That's what I supposed to do, pray for you when you become weak, and even when you're strong."

If my husband would have done it any other way the outcome probably would have gone horribly wrong. I had a big problem with my husband praying but no matter how many times I would attack him, he continued to pray. He did not allow anything or anybody to come between him and God. Although I felt bad for attempting to commit adultery, I was still determined to make him stumble. When I met him he was a thug and I wanted the person that I fell in love with back.

The Fight Was Worth It

I'll Be Your Eve, Just Be My Adam

These Eve tendencies of mine were pushing me further away from God. I was Eve and I was hoping to make him my Adam. My husband and I were constantly in a tug a war. While I was trying to pull him away from Christ, he was trying to pull me back to Christ. I was getting more and more comfortable punching him whenever he said or did something that I did not approve of. Until the day his nephew came over, I call this one, *'Nose Wide Open.'*

I was trying to get my husband's attention but he was sharing my attention with his nephew. I was trying to be cool about it at first but after a while I could not hide it anymore. So, I started walking through the house slamming doors, yelling, just being hateful hoping that my husband noticed my anger. From time to time my husband would come and see after me but then he would go back in there with his nephew. However, what pushed me to my breaking point was when I asked my husband to stay in the room with me, and he said his nephew came over to spend time with him. When my husband made that comment it was like he slammed on my brakes because I snapped.

I hailed a round of punches to his face. I was about to hit him again until I noticed the blood on my sore fist. When I looked at my husband's face, that's when the blood

The Fight Was Worth It

started flowing from his nose, onto his white t-shirt. I could not believe that I just hit my husband in front of our nephew out of a jealous rage. That was the moment I realized it was time for me to change. I apologized to my husband and vowed as long as I lived to never hit him again. For the first six months my wicked ways were lying dormant in my flesh. I was hiding my anger under a doormat of guilt. Although I wanted to ring his neck at times, my guilt would not let me. After a while I was no longer playing behind an Orchestra of guilt. I was now able to lead my emotions by walking away in the midst of anger.

The Fight Was Worth It

Prayer

Lord, I am seeking your guidance and direction
all the day long.
Lord I'd rather do it your way and suffer
instead of doing it my way to gain phony happiness.
Curious where you would take me,
But along the way I hope I find,
Myself more obedient
because doing it any other way I could die.
Not necessarily a natural death but a Spiritual death
if my ways don't line up with Yours.
Lord please forgive me.
Forgive me for being out of order in my deeds and words.
Lord, I just want to say thank You for forgiving me.

The Fight Was Worth It

The Husband and Wife Ministry

Shortly after that we got pregnant with baby number three, Tere'. I was really starting to be a different person. My husband was now able to take interest in other things without getting my wrath, his interest was now music. For our anniversary my mom bought my husband and me our first computer. My husband went out and bought a bunch of software and hardware to make music. He had the slightest idea what to do with it but he said God told him to do it, so he did.

The music stuff collected dust for a longtime. At the time neither one of us had plans of doing anything much more than taking care of our children, working, and pleasing God in every way possible. I was now on board the "good train." My husband was seeking God for his next move. The next thing I knew, my husband wrote and produced his first song. He was so proud when he ministered it to me. The beat was simply "wack," but to him it was a masterpiece. I could not help myself. I laughed at him, my parents laughed at him, his cousins laughed at him, his sister laughed at him, the people at church laughed at him, everybody that heard him rap laughed. As if that was not bad enough, he put me on his next song, and we both got laughed at. I was heated and told him, "I told you this was a stupid idea! What was you thinking? I told you, you can't rap! They laughed at you when you did it by yourself! What was you thinking, they wasn't gone laugh at

The Fight Was Worth It

us if we did it together! You don't even know how to make music! Why would you spend all our money on this music stuff anyway? It was just a waste of time and money! You said this is what God told you to do! So why they laugh at us when we got on stage?" I was yelling so loud I could feel the strain on my heart.

"Baby people are not always going to receive what God tell you to do. It's not about whether they receive it or not. It's about whether you do what God told you to do or not."

"Here you go again with this God stuff! I'm not Jesus! I can't take the persecution! Look, I don't want to do it anymore! So don't ask! Like I said, you can't rap and neither can I!"

"Baby the Lord said for us to do it together, and if you don't, you would be acting out of disobedience. Whether people are for me or against me, I'm going to keep doing it as long as God tells me to. "

So a few days later my husband started playing this beat and our daughter started saying to the beat, "Yes Jesus gonna make a way. Yes Jesus gonna make a way."

My husband hoped up laughing, grabbed our daughter and started hugging her and he said, "That's it, that's it! This is going to be the single!"

Instantly those words ministered to me. No matter what it look like Jesus would make a way. So, I hit the studio and words were just coming to me, and God gave me the title of our group through that song; "Reflections of

The Fight Was Worth It

Christ." Once we did that song for the first time our ministry started picking up. We went all over town doing *'Make a Way.'* We started writing more songs and ministering them but all the people cared about was *'Make A Way.'*

It was like we were local celebrities. We were even offered a deal. I was thinking, 'Man, some people do this for years before they get a deal, and we been doing this less than a year and we got a deal. We must be good.'

I forgot by whom we did this for, and I was knocked off course. I started clashing with the person that signed us because pride started stirring up in me even more. One of the guys on the label and I were lusting after each other. From time to time he would call and we would talk about God and other stuff, but we (and God) knew our motives were not right. I recognized that I was sinning, but I kept talking to him. I was now talking to this new man and the guy that gave me "oral pleasures," all while I was married.

It was as if it didn't bother my husband. He kept forgiving me so I kept doing it. My husband eventually spoke up and said that if I talk to another guy while we are married, our marriage would be over. That's when I cut my extra marital relationships off as quickly as I started them.

I believe I brought a curse upon my family because as the relationship with these guys failed, so did everything else. Even though I was never with either guy alone we still were sinning with the desire for one another in our hearts. My husband and I were no longer on the label. The Lord told us to move out of our home, my van started

The Fight Was Worth It

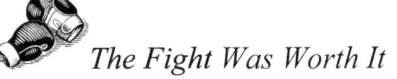

giving us major problems, I got pregnant with our fourth child, and I lost my job. When my husband, our three children, and I moved in with my parents I was eight months pregnant. There were nine people staying in a three bedroom house. This move was drastic for us because at first we had everything. But my pride and attempts at adultery caused everything we had to become like a cracker in a closed fist, because everything we had crumbled.

    Knowing what I had done, my husband and I took a break from the ministry. We started to seek God on a more personal level. I had now given birth to baby number four, William Jr. What a joy! As we were seeking God He started blessing us big time. We were blessed with another place to live, a new vehicle, and God allowed us to have more now than we did when I was working. I was growing with God. I was reading the Word, and I was on track. I was at a point now where nothing was able to separate me from God. Until one day I got distracted by that lustful demon again, but this time it came in the form of a female.

The Fight Was Worth It

ADULTERY AGAIN

My husband and I were about to leave for church when we got a knock on the door. When I opened the door I was stuck like there was glue on the soles of my shoes or something. I could not speak but my mouth was wide open. It was my ex-girlfriend and my family. She was as beautiful as ever to me. She spoke, looked me up and down, walked passed me, and that's when the scent from her body opened my nostrils like the aroma of sweet cinnamon. Whatever she had on caused the hair on the back of my neck to stand up while my mouth watered. Once I shook whatever just happened off, my husband was saying, "Do you hear me? Let's go?"

We went to church like nothing happened. Once we got to church all I could do was pray for her, and try to focus on the service and not her. Here I was with my husband but "tripping off" this girl that was my friend, then lover. This was my first time seeing her in about six years. She left town after I married William because she said she hated that I moved on. She ended up forgiving me about two years earlier. She had come back to visit me and my family, and my feelings for her were reawakened. I was going to keep my distance but during my observation of her at church, it seemed like she was being convicted. Nevertheless, I thought I could reel her in. After service she told me, "I almost didn't wanna be gay no mo."

The Fight Was Worth It

At that point I felt like I could take her under my wing and give her the same guidance that I eventually got. But that decision was like one drunk trying to drive another drunk home without crashing? I was starting to get intoxicated by this lustful spirit. I felt I could shake it though because I had the Holy Spirit. I went to my husband and asked him if I could let her come over so I could mentor her. My husband instantly recognized the plan of the enemy and rejected my request to mentor her. After a heated argument, I assured him that I had the Holy Spirit so I could not stumble. I felt like having the Holy Spirit was my validation for everything. I thought having the Holy Spirit meant I did not have to apply anything else from the Word of God to my life.

However, that way of thinking was cancerous to my soul, and my husband tried telling me that. I told him he was falsely accusing me of lusting for her. We got into another heated argument because I really thought I could not stumble. Things went wrong when I did not submit to my husband. When my husband said he did not want her in our home, I should have respected his request, considering she was my ex. He eventually disagreed, but agreed and said, "I don't think she should come over because it's a trick from the enemy, but gone let her come over."

The first day I let her over my house caused a fire to burn within me. But I wanted to prove my husband wrong so I told him, "See William. I told you. Nothing. When she came over, there was nothing."

"Oh okay. I know differently, but I apologize."

The Fight Was Worth It

She was coming over every day and it seemed like old times without the sex. The more she came over the more I would lust after her hoping she would soon make her move on me. The more I lusted after her the further from God I was getting.

By this time my faith in God was a see-saw. I would be up and excited about God when she was not around, but as soon as she would come around I would fall. After a while I was just down. I would go to church and get prayer because I knew my ways had to change, soon. I was thinking, 'But if I changed now she would never make her move on me, and in a way, I want her to solve my riddle.'

So I would leave church the same way I went in, bound with a heavy burden. I was spiritually fainting. That spirit of lust was crazy. I was lusting after her while hoping the married and single men would lust after me. I was certainly a wolf in sheep's clothing. The enemy was persecuting me, causing me to stay bound. How do I go from worshiping Satan, to getting saved, ministering with my husband, and now back to barely holding on to my faith?

My husband would come home and speak to me about what God showed him, but I would put on my Oscar winning "denial performance." By the time he was finished I would feel spiritually convicted, but physically I craved sensual things. Messing with her was causing all forms of confusion. I wanted to be free but, confusion wouldn't let me. I could not believe I was going through this attempted adultery cycle all over again. I was a seasoned Christian acting as if I did not know the Lord at all.

The Fight Was Worth It

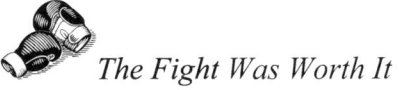

The enemy was feeding me a can of lies. As my church leader was revealing the truth behind my mask of deception, I would hear the enemy telling me not to admit to anything. Plus one of the members already told me she hated homosexuals so why should I admit to this, so they can talk about me? So, I stayed quiet about it, bound, and full of pride. I was praying that no one noticed my extra martial affair, so I tried hard not to look anyone in their eyes. The eyes are the lamp to the soul, and there was pain all in my eyes. I was starting to believe every lie from the enemy, and I was getting weaker every week. My husband said that God wanted me free but I was not accepting correction. I was now as drained as an empty sink. I knew that I could not keep going back and forth like this but my flesh wanted her.

The Fight Was Worth It

Dying to Be Touched by Her

One morning when I got up I had planned to bring my ex-girlfriend to my house but it was put on my heart not too. I told myself that I would not go and get her, but as soon as she called I fell weak, and picked her up.

My husband was working to bring money into the house, while I was working on a plan to sin. I was trying to give her hint after hint that I wanted her, and I was hoping that her motives were just as evil as mine. I started off sitting with my legs open and she said, "Yeah I see it."

I started laughing and said, "See what?"

While thinking, 'Yes she noticed it. Yes she noticed me. Man I want her to touch it so bad!'

She ended up asking me, "Well, can I taste it just one more time?"

Instead of putting her out of my house I sat there and entertained the thought. Then she said, "I am so much better than I was back then."

"Better, wow! You were good back then! Oops I should not said that aloud." My mind started visualizing all kinds of stuff.

"Well can I touch it?" She asked.

The Fight Was Worth It

And I told her, "Man I want you too so bad but I know I can't."

"Well, won't no body know but us."

"My husband would."

She asked, "How?"

And I said, "Because I will tell him."

She started laughing, "Girl you is crazy. What you trying to do, get busted over the head with something?"

"My husband is not gone hit me."

"Well don't tell him and he won't know."

"I want you so bad I could almost feel it, but I don't want to curse my family."

"I would make it worth it KeeKee."

"Really? Man, I know what you can do and man oh man, but I don't want to lose everything. But I do want you!"

"Girl, look, you might as well let me do it. You thought about it."

"So. What does that mean?"

"It's in your heart girl, so it's like you did it anyway."

"You right, so come on."

The Fight Was Worth It

She hopped up and asked, "Are you serious?"

"Yeah."

She started coming towards me. I started laughing and hopped up. "I'm just playing girl. I'm not trying to lose everything I have. I love my husband. I want you, but I love my husband."

Once again I was tempted to commit adultery. By that time my leader called and asked me if everything was okay. I told her it was, and she asked me if I was sure and I told her yeah. Then she said she was feeling something and that's when I confessed. She told me to get that girl out my house right away and never invite her over again. Then she told me to pray over my house and tell my husband everything.

I had a sexual demon on me that had me thinking, dreaming, and thirsting after sexual attention. That spirit manifested itself to destroy the ministry that God had ordained for my husband and me. I was looking with my natural eyes, so at the time I did not realize that I was looking for pleasure in all the wrong places. If I was not having sex, thinking about sex, or talking about sex it was like my body would go into shock. It was like I was a diabetic, and sex was my insulin. I was on a downward spiral toward destruction because being sinful was becoming easy for me.

The Word says a double minded man is unstable in all his ways. I was double minded and it laid a red carpet of confusion out before me. My life had been full of confusion. But now I was even more confused. I looked like I had it all together, but on the inside of me was a boiling stew of lies. Spiritually and mentally I was dying. Physically, I was ready to satisfy my sinful nature at any cost. I was on the verge of a meltdown. However, through that incident God showed me the importance of reading His Word. The Word is rejuvenating to our spirit, so we need it. The word tells us to keep our minds on Christ and he would keep us in perfect peace. I had no peace. Much of this stuff so easily crept into my life because I did not keep myself equipped with the word of God. Just as we need natural food daily, the same holds true with spiritual food. I was as off balance as a table with three legs.

The Fight Was Worth It

The Dismembered Body

After speaking with my leader I was able to recognize the errors in my ways, but I did not know how to change. I realized that my disobedience to my husband was taking a toll on him, myself, our home, and our ministry. There were many days I would have to pray for God's strength to have the desire to do God's will, but change was not coming fast enough. There were times where I would do great but that desire for evil things would always come back.

This back and forth struggle with my faith was tearing me down. I curled up in the fetal position wanting to die. I had a hard time separating my past from my present. When I would mess up I could not forget about it, or forgive myself. I would walk the streets of shame, while other times I would be drowning in the pool of guilt. Instead of running to the church I wanted to run away from it. I thought everybody knew what I had done. My husband was a great support system for me in spite of what I had done. He was not about to stand by and watch as I drowned without pulling me out to safety. Praying for me and keeping me connected to the body, was that safe place.

Once I got there, all the reasons why I didn't want to go to church in the first place became my reality. If God, the one that sent his only begotten Son to die for the sin of all mankind could forgive us so easily, how come those that are made in God's likeness can't forgive? I had messed up

The Fight Was Worth It

but they were acting like I sinned against them. Other than my immediate family and three others, no one was showing me love at church. I would be at church amongst other members of the body, but I felt alone, and disconnected. At my church, we speak then hug before and after service, but to add sorrow on top of burden, I was the pink elephant in the room. Some people would even turn their noses up at me. Others were rolling their eyes at me. If I would tell certain members, "I loved you."

They would say, "Me too."

I was thinking, 'Wow! Really? In the church? What happened to I love you too?' As if that was not bad enough, they would stand before the church and say, "If anybody's feeling like nobody loves them that's just the enemy," and I got to thinking, 'Wow! Really in the church. Why every time something happens with me they want to address the church? I thought love was something you could feel. I don't feel nothing but hatred from these people. I hate coming here, I hate it!'

Instead of praying for me, some people were talking about me. I knew because either someone would tell me or I would overhear it. When I could not pray for myself I needed them to pray for me. They were so busy talking bad about me that they were missing the fact that they were out of order too. There were other times I would ask for prayer and I would get pushed away and told to pray for myself. That's when I got to thinking, 'Yeah I do have to pray for myself, but until I get to that point, I need y'all praying for me. I need y'all coming in agreement on my behalf for God to turn some things around in my life. But right now, here I

The Fight Was Worth It

am thinking about killing somebody or myself, and you telling me to pray for myself. Come on!'

I needed to be delivered soon. I was like a ticking time bomb-not knowing when I would explode into a sinful rage. At the same time doing right was a struggle because it was like walking on ice. I did not know how much longer I would be able to hold on. When I got into my feelings I cared less about what others thought. Because of my guilt, I was ready to walk away from the church forever.

The Fight Was Worth It

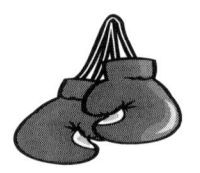

Dear God

It has happened again. My unending tears are falling. I have stepped out of my box only to be rejected again. What is this struggle that I am experiencing? Lord it just seems like I can't win! God these people act like I don't have feelings. God I want to punch this wall and scream so they will hear me…But he or she won't care. I refrain from saying their names because I don't want to bring them shame. God I have been rejected so long. It's like nobody finds anything in me worth getting along with. I'm flinching like I'm a crack fiend because I want to go into attack mode. Lord, take that desire away from me because I really don't want to attack anymore; I'm just hurting. I know I have sinned and fallen short of doing your will, but God help me!

The Fight Was Worth It

Like A Table with Three Legs

Here I was seeing no point in praying anymore because the church scarred me. My mind was made up. I was not going to pray, read my bible, or go to church anymore. I was done. Inside and outside of church, I would hear my husband praying for me. I would see my husband crying out to God on my behalf. It would have been so much easier for my husband to walk away. My husband said I was his wife and he was willing to fight for my soul until either I was won over, or God called him home. My husband was not going to give up or walk away from his family.

I asked him to leave many times and explained to him how I felt about our ministry and the church. But one time he told me, "When I made my vows before God I meant it. I can't leave when things get hard. I have to pray harder. You can't leave the church because you feel like people are mistreating you and even if they are, we have to let God handle that. And concerning the ministry, if you feel like you are not getting the recognition that you desire, just know everything we do should be unto God. As long as you are pleasing Him that is all that matters. No matter how much I have to pray or fast, no matter how hard it gets; no matter what you put me through, I am not going to walk away from my wife and children. It does get hard but I love God first and my family enough to stand on God's Word that He will save my whole household. Baby this is just a test to be added to our testimony, and we are going to make it through this together."

After that speech I was in tears. My husband only saw me cry one other time eight years earlier. There was snot rolling into my mouth. I was huffing and puffing. I laid my head on his shoulder, and he was crying too. If I had ever questioned my husband's love before, that was the defining moment that clearly revealed his love for me. At that moment my husband became more than just my husband and the father of our children. My husband became my best friend. My husband was going through the most but he never gave upon me. I did not esteem myself enough to believe I could stay saved, but my husband did. He saw something in me that I did not see in myself.

"I understand everything that you are saying. But when I mess up, in my mind I have failed. I am so used to failing that sometimes I don't even try to do what's right. William, I am so unworthy of the titles wife, mother, and Christian because I don't know what's required of me. But, I will try to do better."

"No, you are not unworthy because if you were, God would not have given you those titles."

I felt convicted enough to move forward into my destiny. Not too long after that I got pregnant with baby number five, Arvontez Bronze. Then, God blessed us with a bigger home. My husband and I were still not doing our rap ministry but we were giving our testimonies. We were still going through our share of trials but we were praying, fasting, and reading the Word. We gained strength in our

The Fight Was Worth It

weakest hours. The Lord then spoke to my husband and told him that it was time for him to become a solo artist. Seemingly right after that confirmation, I started having all kinds of pregnancy complications. I again stopped reading my Word because I was overwhelmed. I was working, going to school, trying to be a wife and mother, plus studying, and when I wasn't doing any of that I was sleeping. I had my share of ups and downs during that pregnancy, but once I delivered my son I was delivered of those issues that were holding me back. God then spoke to me that it was time for me to minister in the form of spoken word. I did not know where to start but God said to write, and that's what I did. The next thing I knew, God blessed me to travel doing spoken word.

The Fight Was Worth It

Prayer Request

Lord, this morning when I got up I didn't start my day with you. Instead, the first thing that greeted me was my set of problems from yesterday. I thought the more I worried about my problems things would change. Instead, things got worse. Lord, I had to realize that it is not worry that will change my problems, but I must trust in you. Lord, I know you are interceding on my behalf to the Father, daily. I know the Father will grant me the desires of my heart as long as I am in good standings with Him. I don't have to be perfect but I must not be effortless either. You said if I had faith as small as a mustard seed I would be able to move mountains. Lord, grant me that faith because I am ready for a change. Lord, I know faith without works is dead, so give me the strength to work my faith, in Jesus name.

God, I realize that I can't do it without you. I believe you are able to bring me through any hard trial, because you live. Your Word says, you are the same yesterday, today, and forever more, and I believe that! God I am trusting in you to bring me and my family through. Lord, I had given up only because I didn't know what to do anymore. But I heard in my spirit "Pray, pray, pray." I heard you telling me you are using these very situations for my ministry.

The Fight Was Worth It

Lord wow! I was just looking at me, my circumstances, my own emotions and not realizing that You are preparing me. God the way you do stuff I sometimes just don't understand, but I thank you for understanding me. You understand me when I sometimes don't understand me. God forgive me for complaining. God forgive me for not knowing how to love my husband and children. God forgive me for wanting to commit adultery. Forgive me for not forgiving other. Forgive me for hurting others intentionally. God forgive me for hurting others with the intent to kill. And God please, please forgive me for the day I was ready to walk away.

The Fight Was Worth It

A River of Tears

I decided the rocks would not have to cry out for me anymore. I started praying for myself. Even when I did not want to read the Word of God, I read it anyway. I started to feel strength come back to my body. I felt rejuvenated. I felt like I was ready to climb the mountain of obstacles that was placed before me, instead of being over taken by the lava. I was going to plead with God for myself. I got off my butt. I got down on my knees and cried out to God, for the first time in a very long time.

I told myself that I was going to stop dictating my own walk with Christ based on how others treated me. I've learned that misery loves company and if you give space to the enemy, he'll take over.

This time, instead of going back and forth with the enemy I picked up my baggage, took it to the altar, and emptied it there. I decided at that very moment that I was going to build my personal relationship with God. I realized that with every test God wanted to see how qualified I was for the next level-in Him. Sometimes I would fail the test, other times I would pass the test. There were many days that I would get so caught up in my situations that I would forget what my God is capable of. However, when I thought about what God delivered me from, I would rejoice. I was now at a point in my life where I was able to hold on to God's unchanging hand. I had made up my mind to serve God until the day I die. So whenever my problems

The Fight Was Worth It

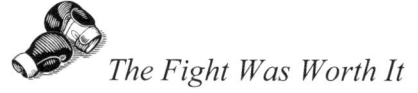

would become bigger than me, I would start praising God, praying, and fasting if needed, because this time I was not giving up!

The Fight Was Worth It

His Voice

It was just a whisper
And extremely hard to be heard

The essence of His voice
Sang out to my heart
Like the sweetest melodies of a bird

As I sat there and listened
I was hearing this voice in my head

But this time it was different
It wasn't telling me I was better off dead

So I would go on with my life
But I could not act the same
Cause the more I would want to sin
Just the thought of it brought shame

I didn't know what was going on
Why I felt so strange
But something happened the day
I called on Christ's Name
I didn't know I was ready
I didn't know I could change
But as long as I allow Your Spirit to guide
My life would never be the same
Glory be to God!

The Fight Was Worth It

Psalms 15: 1-5 (NLT)

Who may worship in your sanctuary, Lord?
Who may enter your presence on your holy hill?
Those who lead blameless lives and do what is right,
speaking the truth from sincere hearts.
Those who refuse to gossip
or harm their neighbors
or speak evil of their friends.
Those who despise flagrant sinners,
and honor the faithful followers of the Lord,
and keep their promises even when it hurts.
Those who lend money without charging interest,
and who cannot be bribed to lie about the innocent.
Such people will stand firm forever. I desire to be looked at by God as one of His faithful.

The Fight Was Worth It

The Trick of the Enemy

Previously the devil tricked me into believing he was my friend. He tricked me into believing that everybody was against me, and yes I even believed my husband was against me. He tricked me into believing that if I worshipped him I would have all things, and be able to do anything. The devil tricked me into believing I was just being me, so I was no sinner. I now know that he lied because he can't give me power that he does not have.

I lived through the lies of the enemy for so long. The truth of the situation is that the devil plans were to kill me, but God saw fit for me to live! The devil tricked me into believing that Jesus was the enemy. As long as I was unable to call on Jesus, the devil was able to dwell within me. I am now able to call on Jesus, so the devil had to flee, including his residue. Not only that, but he was trying to destroy my marriage because he hated that William and I were going to stand together in ministry. He diligently tried stopping us. He hates that I am now able to look in the mirror and see that I am a creation of God. He hates that I am now able to love myself for who I am. I know that I am freed because of Christ.

The Fight Was Worth It

A PIECE OF ME

Horror at the door
A piece of me he's trying to take

The joy of this feeling is far from the love we make
Tears in my eyes, and my voice is far from spoken

Memories I have to endure and after every thought
I am choking…

Pierced my ego and embarrassed the family's name
Piece by piece he takes a part of me
Even though I want him to stop he won't
Why, I can't explain

Love, a four letter word
And hate is too
Irresponsible you were
When you took a piece of me with you

Why question it
You don't even have to explain
This dismay of an affair
My prize possession you tried to obtain

So distant from you
But yet we connect in the worse way

The Fight Was Worth It

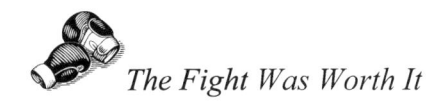

I hated you
I hated you because of what you did to me
Because you changed my whole life
The day you took a piece of me

You took a piece of me and never once said I love you
You took a piece of me and never once did I hug you
You took a piece of me and often we had words
But only if I knew what I would go through
You, I never would have served

You would never understand because of who you are
How much it hurt
THAT DAY WHEN YOU TOOK A PIECE OF ME
In the palm of your hands!

The Fight Was Worth It

Dear God

God you are my light in dark places. Not dark places I go, but in dark times in my life. God you are the light that led me through my darkest hours. When I was ready to give up, you were the light that showed me the path to follow. God you have shown me that I am something even though I thought I was nothing. God I have never yearned after you as I do today. I am now at a place of true repentance, led by your light. God there were times that I questioned your plans for me. God but Luke 1:37 tell me 'for with God nothing shall be impossible'. God I thank you for lighting a path for me that led me from darkness.

The Fight Was Worth It

From the Dark Side to Christ

As of the day I rededicated my life to Christ, the duration of the battle with my flesh verses the spirit was eight years. As God promised, He did not leave me or forsake me. However, there were many days that my pride interfered with my faith walk, but I knew in my heart that I needed more. The Word of God reads in James 5:16, 'Confess your faults one to another, and pray one for another, that ye may be healed. The effectual fervent prayer of a righteous man availeth much.' Matthew 17:21, 'Howbeit this kind goeth not out but by prayer and fasting.' I thank God for my parents, my husband, and our leaders that would pray and fast for us. I am now delivered of those issues that kept me bound for so long. I was able to write this book out of obedience to God, so that He could use my testimony to begin a healing process for someone else. I am unashamed of my past.

I can say from experience that we really do serve a loving, caring, and forgiving God. Other than blasphemy against the Holy Spirit and not forgiving others, there is no sin too great that God won't forgive you of. I've tried just about everything, even selling my soul to the devil, but God delivered me from it all. I will say this, living as a Christian is a fight, but the fight is worth it.

When I look back on where my husband and I come from, and here we are today, I have to give God all the glory because He kept us together. If it was not for God

The Fight Was Worth It

who is by our side, where would we be? William could have killed me, or I him, or we could have killed each other. Glory be to God that we are still here as a testament of what our God can do. God is doing a tremendous transformation in our lives.

Today my husband is an ordained minister and my best friend. We do ministry together and God has blessed us with five children. Put no limit on what God can do, what He has done for us, He can do the same for you. What the devil meant for our harm, God has turned around, and we glorify Him today. We are not yet perfect, but daily we are striving for perfection.

The Fight Was Worth It

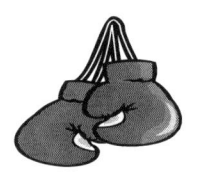

Psalms 116: 1-14 (NLT)

I love the Lord because he hears my voice
and my prayer for mercy.
Because he bends down to listen,
I will pray as long as I have breath!
Death wrapped its ropes around me;
the terrors of the grave overtook me.
I saw only trouble and sorrow.
Then I called on the name of the Lord:
"Please, Lord, save me!"
How kind the Lord is! How good he is!
So merciful, this God of ours!
The Lord protects those of childlike faith;
I was facing death, and he saved me.
Let my soul be at rest again,
for the Lord has been good to me.
He has saved me from death,
my eyes from tears,
my feet from stumbling.
And so I walk in the Lord's presence
as I live here on earth!
I believed in you, so I said,
"I am deeply troubled, Lord."
In my anxiety I cried out to you,
"These people are all liars!"
What can I offer the Lord
for all he has done for me?
I will lift up the cup of salvation
and praise the Lord's name for saving me.

The Fight Was Worth It

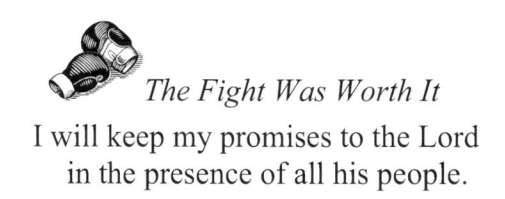

I will keep my promises to the Lord
in the presence of all his people.

The Fight Was Worth It

The Funeral

This is my funeral
And I am looking out into the world
With new eyes
Unable to move or speak like them anymore
Because that part of me is dead.
I have risen with Christ
But mine is not the resurrection
It's just me going to another level in Him,
Which I call a blessing.
At first I refused to die to myself
And I almost missed out
On the celebrations of life that Joseph talked about,
Christ.
Before my death to this world
Accomplishments that I wanted
Were far from me accomplishing
Because the death of My Self esteem
Caused the birth of Hindrance.
I was buried up to my eyes
With no hope, depression, pain and fear
Jealousy, doubt and I was apprehensive to hear
Because I couldn't see anything pass the misery I had here.

I was so trustworthy in death
Because I knew it had me.

The Fight Was Worth It

I was like a tin man because I had no heart.
I was as cold as the winter wind
Having no love for myself or for Christ.
I kept rejecting Christ because even when he was near
I still felt like he was far from me.
Until it took an inner view of death
The day it tried to consume me.

But by faith today I do trust God,
And today I celebrate the funeral of Laziness
I was too lazy to stand for God.
Today I celebrate the funeral of Disobedience toward God
Because at first if I could not see it coming to pass I would not do it.
But today I will trust God and do just what he says.

Today I celebrate the funeral of Envy, because there is no need for me to envy because what God has for me is for me, what God has for you is for you, and instead of envying your blessing, I too should be rejoicing with you.
Today I celebrate the funeral of Fear, Jealousy, Insecurities and Low Self- esteem
I will now look in the mirror and see a queen because I am part of God's creation.
Today I celebrate the funeral of Me Saying I Am Nothing because again, I'm part of His creation and when He created me He created something.
In the past my negativity about my own accomplishments were suffocating me. I often failed to try because I feared I would fail. Today, I celebrate the funeral of Not Trying and Being So Swift To Give Up because hard work pays off.
I was paralyzed in agonizing pain because even though I wanted too, I couldn't, because I didn't know how to succeed.
Because success was incomprehensible to me

The Fight Was Worth It

But today
Today I want to say goodbye to all those things.
Those things that had me bound.
The things that I have not achieved
I want to say hello to because it's my new season.
No longer will I fail to try
But I will outlive my dreams
Because the day I realized Christ as my guide
Was the day I omitted my way
And made Christ the One in which I'm allied

The Fight Was Worth It

THE TONGUE

Y'all my God is my strength and my deliverer. When I seek Him daily who shall I fear? Many have risen up against me but God has delivered me from them all. I seek God because there is no one else that I could trust. I have tried to put my trust in man but they fail me more than they console me. My strength is in God. He has given me power over the enemy. God has entrusted me with what could be a deadly poison. I can use it to bless or curse men at my leisure. I can speak life over my situation or destroy the course of it by speaking death. Therefore, I must use wisdom when speaking to God and people. I refuse to give up and so I declare victory over every situation in my life that has come to destroy me. There is power in the tongue!

The Fight Was Worth It

"WARNING"

By

Kashe'la Armstead

Don't look at you but look at God

He died for you and gave His only Son

Don't turn back

Don't allow the devil to defeat you

When you're under attack God is strong

He does not want us to do wrong

Look unto the hills

In which come your help

So chill out

Call on God's name

Look to the Lord and don't give up

Try to understand His words and try to comprehend

We should not do wrong

Believe in God

That's what I say because God's way is the right way!

The Fight Was Worth It

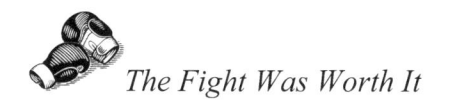

Thank You

To everyone that purchased my book, thank you. To my mom Freda and dad Ollie, I love you so much. Mom and Dad you have been through so much with me but you never gave up on me, even when I wanted to give up on myself. I would never be able to express in words or deeds how much I appreciate, love, and thank you for all you have done and still do.

I want to thank my husband and children for everything. I love you all very much! I would not have a book without your encouragement.

I remember the first time my mom read my manuscript aloud. One of my babies asked was the story true and I said yes, then all my babies started hugging me and crying. Moments like that I will never forget, priceless.

I would like to thank you Jesus for allowing me to live and not die. I thank you for giving me the strength to be courageous enough to share my testimony. I love you Jesus and through you, I am truly blessed.

The Fight Was Worth It

The Fight Was Worth It